HANDBOOK OF NATURE STUDY:

GARDEN FLOWERS, TREES

COMPLETE YOUR COLLECTION TODAY!

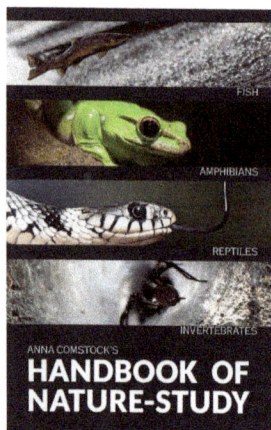

REPTILES, AMPHIBIANS,
FISH AND INVERTEBRATES

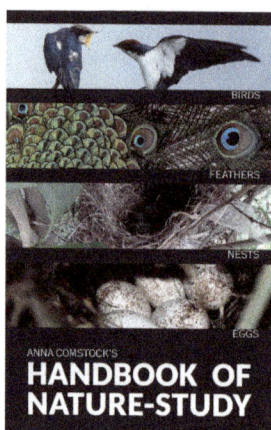

BIRDS

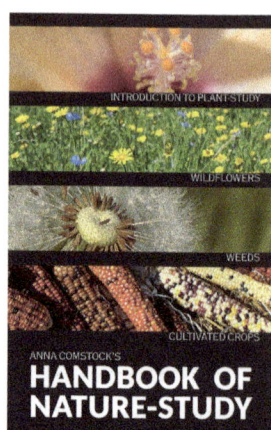

WILDFLOWERS, WEEDS
AND CULTIVATED CROPS

MAMMALS AND
FLOWERLESS PLANTS

TREES AND
GARDEN FLOWERS

EARTH AND SKY

INSECTS

INTRODUCTION

Handbook of
Nature-Study:
Garden Flowers and Trees

ANNA BOTSFORD COMSTOCK, B.S., L.H.D

LATE PROFESSOR OF NATURE-STUDY IN CORNELL UNIVERSITY

LIVING BOOK
PRESS

This edition published 2020
by Living Book Press

Copyright © Living Book Press, 2020

ISBN: 978-1-922348-66-1 (hardcover)
         978-1-922348-67-8 (softcover)

A catalogue record for this book is available from the National Library of Australia

CONTENTS

GARDEN FLOWERS

TREES

GARDEN FLOWERS

The Crocus

TEACHER'S STORY

THE crocus, like the snowdrop, cannot wait for the snow to be off the ground before it pushes up its gay blossoms, and it has thus earned the gratitude of those who are winter weary.

The crocus has a corm instead of a bulb like the snowdrop or daffodil. A corm is a solid, thickened, underground stem, and is not in layers, like the onion. The roots come off the lower side of the corm. The corm of the crocus is well wrapped in several, usually five, white coats with papery tips. When the plant begins to grow the leaves push up through the coats. The leaves are grasslike and may be in number from two to eight, depending on the variety. Each leaf has its edge folded, and the white midrib has a plait on either side, giving it the appearance of being box-plaited on the under

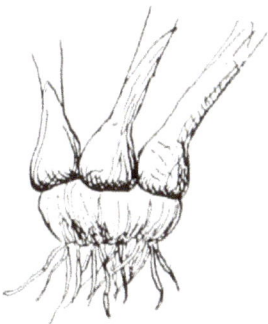

The old and young corms of the crocus

3

side. The bases of the leaves enclosed in the corm coats are yellow, since they have had no sunlight to start their starch factories and the green within their cells. At the center of the leaves appear the blossom buds, each enclosed in a sheath.

The petals and sepals are similar in color, but the three sepals are on the outside, and their texture, especially on the outer side, is coars-

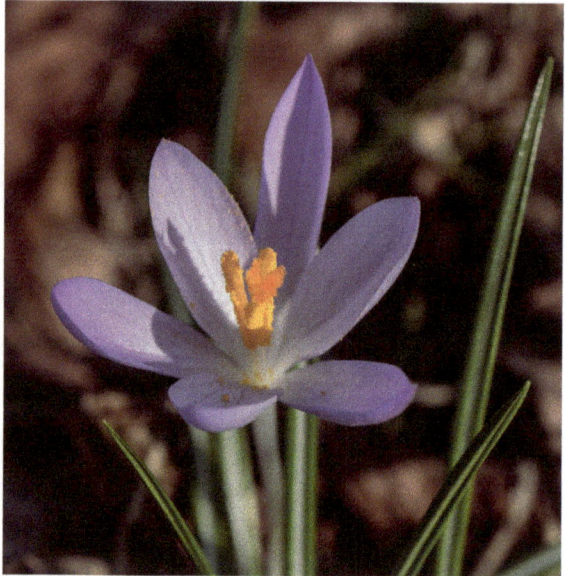

A crocus close up

er than that of the three protected petals. But sepals and petals unite into a long tube at the base. At the very base of this corolla tube, away down out of sight, even below the surface of the ground, is the seed-box, or ovary. From the tip of the ovary the style extends up through the corolla-tube and is tipped with a ruffled three-lobed stigma.

The three stamens are set at the throat of the corolla tube. The anthers are very long and open along the sides. The anthers mature first, and shed their pollen in the cup of the blossom where any insect, seeking the nectar in the tube of the corolla, must become dusted with it. However, if the stigma lobes fail to get pollen from other flowers, they later spread apart and curl over until they reach some of the pollen of their own flower.

Crocus blossoms have varied colors: white, yellow, orange, purple, the latter often striped or feather-veined. And, while many seeds like tiny pearls, are developed in the oblong capsule, yet it is chiefly by its corms that the crocus multiplies. On top of the mother corm of this year develop several small corms, each capable of growing a plant next year. But after two years of this second-story sort of multiplication the young crocuses are pushed above the surface of the ground.

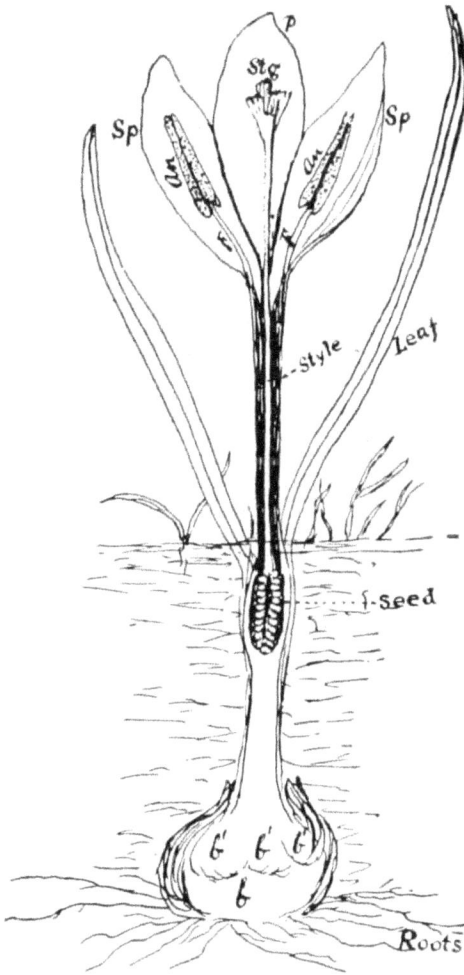

The crocus.
p. petal; sp. sepal; an. anther; f. filament; stg. stigma;
b. mother corm; b' b' b'. young corms.

Thus, they need to be replanted every two or three years. Crocuses may be planted from the first of October until the ground freezes. They make pretty borders to garden beds and paths. Or they may be planted in lawns without disturbing the grass, by punching a hole with a stick or dibble and dropping in a corm and then pressing back the soil in place above it. The plants will mature before the grass needs to be mowed.

LESSON

Leading thought— The crocuses appear so early in the spring, because they have food stored in underground storehouses. They multiply by seeds and by corms.

Method— If it is possible to have crocuses in boxes in the schoolroom windows, the flowers may thus best be studied. Otherwise, when crocuses are in bloom bring them into the schoolroom, bulbs and all, and place them where the children may study them at leisure.

Observations—

1. At what date in the spring have you found crocuses in blossom? Why are they able to blossom so much earlier than other flowers?

2. Take a crocus just pushing up out of its bulb. How many overcoats protect its leaves? What is at the very center of the bulb? Has the flower bud a special overcoat?

A white crocus

3. Describe the leaves. How are they folded in their overcoats? What color are they where they have pushed out above their overcoats? What color are they within the overcoats? Why?

4. Do the flowers or the leaves have stems, or do they arise directly from the bulb?

5. What is the shape of the open crocus flower? Can you tell the difference between sepals and petals in color? Can you tell the difference by their position? Or by their texture above or below? As you look into the flower, which make the points of the triangle, the sepals or the petals?

6. Describe the anthers. How long are they? How many are there? How do they open? What is the color of the pollen? Describe how a bee becomes dusted with pollen. Why does the bee visit the crocus blossom? If she finds nectar there, where is it?

7. Describe the stigma. Open a flower and see how long the style is. How do the sepals and petals unite to protect the style? Where is the seed-box? Is it so far down that it is below ground? How many seeds are developed from a single blossom?

8. How many colors do you find in the crocus flowers? Which are the prettiest in the lawn? Which, in the flower beds?

9. How do the crocus blossoms act in dark and stormy weather? When do they open? How does this benefit them?

10. How do the crocus bulbs multiply? Why do they lift themselves out of the ground and thus need resetting?

11. Describe how to raise crocuses best; the kind of soil, the time of planting, and the best situations.

Out of the frozen earth below,
Out of the melting of the snow,
　　No flower, but a film, I push to light;
No stem, no bud—yet I have burst
The bars of winter, I am the first
　　O Sun, to greet thee out of the night!

Deep in the warm sleep underground
Life is still, and the peace profound:
　　Yet a beam that pierced, and a thrill that smote
Call'd me and drew me from far away;
I rose, I came, to the open day
　　I have won, unshelter'd, alone, remote.

—"THE CROCUS," HARRIET E. H. KING.

When first the crocus thrusts its point of gold,
Up through the still snow-drifted garden-mould,
And folded green things in dim woods unclose
Their crinkled spears, a sudden tremor goes
Into my veins and makes me kith and kin
To every wild-born thing that thrills and blows.

—"A TOUCH OF NATURE," T. B. ALDRICH.

Crocus, the harbinger of spring!

The Daffodils and Their Relatives

"Daffydown Dilly came up in the cold from the brown mold,
Although the March breezes blew keen in her face,
Although the white snow lay on many a place."

THUS, it is that Miss Warner's stanzas tell us the special reason we so love the daffodils. They bring the sunshine color to the sodden earth, when the sun is chary of his favors in our northern latitude; and the sight of the daffodils floods the spirit with a sense of sunlight.

The daffodils and their relatives, the jonquils and narcissus, are interesting when we stop to read their story in their form. The six segments of the perianth, or, as we would say, the three bright-colored sepals and the three inner petals of the flower, are different in shape; but they all look like petals and stand out in star-shape around the flaring end of the flower tube, which, because of its shape, is called the corona, or crown; however, it looks more like a stiff little petticoat extending out in the middle of the flower than it does like a crown. The crown is simply the widened end of the tube of the flower, as may be seen by opening a flower lengthwise; the six seeming petals will peel off the tube, showing that they are fastened to the outside of it. When we look down into the crown of one of these flowers, we see the long style with its three-lobed stigma pushing out beyond the anthers, which are pressed close about it at the throat of the tube; between each two anthers may be seen a little deep passage, through which the tongues of the moth or butterfly can be thrust to reach the nectar. In a tube, slit open, we can see the nectar at the very bottom of it, and it is sweet to the taste and has a decided flavor. In this open tube we may see that the filaments of the stamens are grown fast to the sides of the tube for much of their length, enough remaining free to press the anthers close to the style. The ovary of the pistil is a green swelling at the base of the tube; by cutting it across we can see it is triangular in outline, and has a little cavity in each angle large enough to hold two rows of the little, white, shining, unripe seeds. Each of these cavities is partitioned from the others by a green wall; the partition is marked by a suture on the outside of the seed-pod.

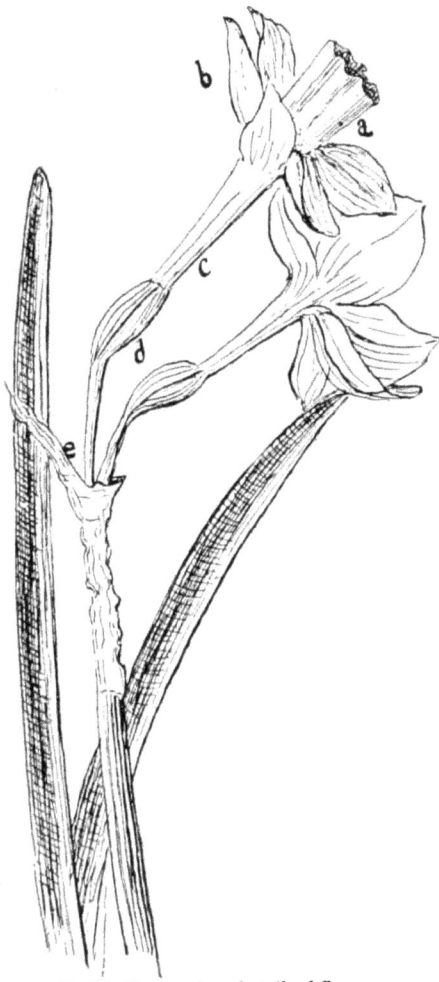

Daffodil showing detail of flower.
a. corona or crown; b. sepals and petals forming perianth; c. corolla tube; d. ovary or seed-case; e. sheath or spathe.

When the flower stalk first appears, it comes up like a sheathed sword, pointing toward the zenith, green, veined lengthwise, and with a noticeable thickening at each edge. As the petals grow, the sheath begins to round out; and then as if to confuse those people who are so stupid as to believe that plants do not really do things, the stiff stem at the base of the sheath bends at right angles. This brings a strain upon the sheath which bursts it, usually along the upper side, although sometimes it tears it off completely at the base.

Narcissus 'Ice_Follies'

The slitted sheath, or spathe, hangs around the stem, wrinkled and parchment-like, very like the loose wrist of a suede glove. The stalk is a strong green tube; the leaves are fleshy and are grooved on the inner side, the groove being deep enough to clasp part way around the flower stem. The number of leaves varies with the variety, and they are usually as tall as the flower stalk. There is one flower on a stalk in the daffodils and the poet's narcissus, but the jonquils and paper-white narcissus have two or more flowers on the same stalk.

A bed should be prepared by digging deep and fertilizing with stable manure. The bulbs should be planted in September or early October, and should be from four to six inches apart, the upper end of the bulbs at least four inches below the surface of the soil. They should not be disturbed but allowed to occupy the bed for a number of years, or as long as they give plenty of flowers. As soon as the surface of the ground is frozen in the winter, the beds should be covered from four to six inches in depth with straw-mixed stable manure, which can be raked off very early in the spring.

The new bulbs are formed at the sides of the old one; for this reason the daffodils will remain permanently planted, and do not lift themselves out of the ground like the crocuses. The leaves of the plant should be allowed to stand as long as they will after the flowers have disappeared, so that they may furnish the bulbs with plenty of food for storing. The seeds should not be allowed to ripen, as it costs the plant too much energy and thus robs the bulbs. The flowers should be cut just as they are opening. Of the white varieties, the poet's narcissus is the most satisfactory, as it is very hardy and very pretty, its corona being a shallow, flaring, greenish yellow rosette with orange-red border, the anthers of its three longest stamens making a pretty center. No wonder Narcissus bent over the pool in joy at viewing himself, if he was as beautiful a man as the poet's narcissus is as a flower.

LESSON

Leading thought—The daffodil, jonquil and narcissus are very closely related, and quite similar. They all come from bulbs which should be planted in September; but after the first planting, they will flower on year after year, bringing much brightness to the gardens in the early spring.

Method—The flowers brought to school may be studied for form, and there should be a special study of the way the flower develops its seed, and how it is propagated by bulbs. The work should lead directly to an interest in the cultivation of the plants. In seedsmen's catalogues or other books, the children will find methods of planting and cultivating these flowers in cities. Daffodils are especially adapted for both window gardens and school gardens.

Observations—

1. Note the shape of the flower. Has it any sepals? What do we call the flowers that have their sepals colored like petals, thus forming a part of the beauty of the flower? Can you see any difference in color, position and texture between the petals and sepals?

2. How do the petal-like parts of these flowers look? How many of them are there? Do they make the most showy part of the flower?

3. What does the central part of the flower look like? Why is it called the corona, or crown? Is it a part of the tube which joins the flower to the stem? Do the petals and sepals peel off this tube? Peel them off one flower, and see that the tube is shaped like a trumpet.

4. Look down into the crown of the flower and tell what you see. Can you see where the insect's tongue must go to reach the nectar?

5. Cut open a trumpet lengthwise to find where the nectar is. How far is it from the mouth of the tube? How long would the insect's tongue have to be to reach it? What insects have tongues as long as this?

6. In order to reach the nectar how would an insect become dusted with pollen? Are the stamens loose in the flower-tube? Is the pistil longer than the stamens? How many parts to the stigma? Can you see how the flowers are arranged so that insects can carry pollen from flower to flower?

7. What is the green swelling in the stem at the base of the trumpet? Is it connected with the style? Cut it across and describe what you see. How do the young seeds look and how are they arranged?

8. Where the flower stem joins the stalk, what do you see? What is this dry spathe there for? Are there one or more flower stems coming from this spathe?

9. Describe the flower stalk. Are the leaves wide or narrow? Are they as long as the flower stalk, are they flat, or are they grooved to fit around the flower stalk?

10. What are the differences between daffodils, jonquils and poet's narcissus? When should the bulbs for these flowers be planted? Will there be more bulbs formed around the one you plant? Will the same bulb ever send up flowers and leaves again? How do the bulbs divide to make new bulbs?

11. How should the bed for the bulbs be prepared? How near together should the bulbs be planted? How deep in the earth? How protect them in the North during the winter?

12. Why should you not cut the leaves off after the flowers have died? Why should you not let the seeds ripen? When should the flowers be cut for bouquets? Who was Narcissus, and why should these early spring flowers be named after him?

Supplementary reading— *Green Things Growing*, Mulock; *The Daffodils*, Wordsworth; *The Story of Narcissus*, Child's Study of the Classics; *Mary's Garden*, Duncan, Chapters XXVI and XXVII.

"I emphatically deny the common notion that the farm boy's life is drudgery. Much of the work is laborious, and this it shares with all work that is productive; for the easier the job the less it is worth doing. But every piece of farm work is also an attempt to solve a problem, and therefore it should have its intellectual interest; and the problems are as many as the hours of the day and as varied as the face of nature.

It needs but the informing of the mind and the quickening of the imagination to raise any constructive work above the level of drudgery. It is not mere dull work to follow the plow—I have followed it day after day—if one is conscious of all the myriad forces that are set at work by the breaking of the furrow; and there is always the landscape, the free fields, the clean soil, the rain, the promise of the crops. Of all men's labor, the farmer's is the most creative.

I cannot help wondering why it is that men will eagerly seek work in the grease and grime of a noisy factory, but will recoil at what they call the dirty work of the farm. So much are we yet bound by tradition!"

—L. H. BAILEY.

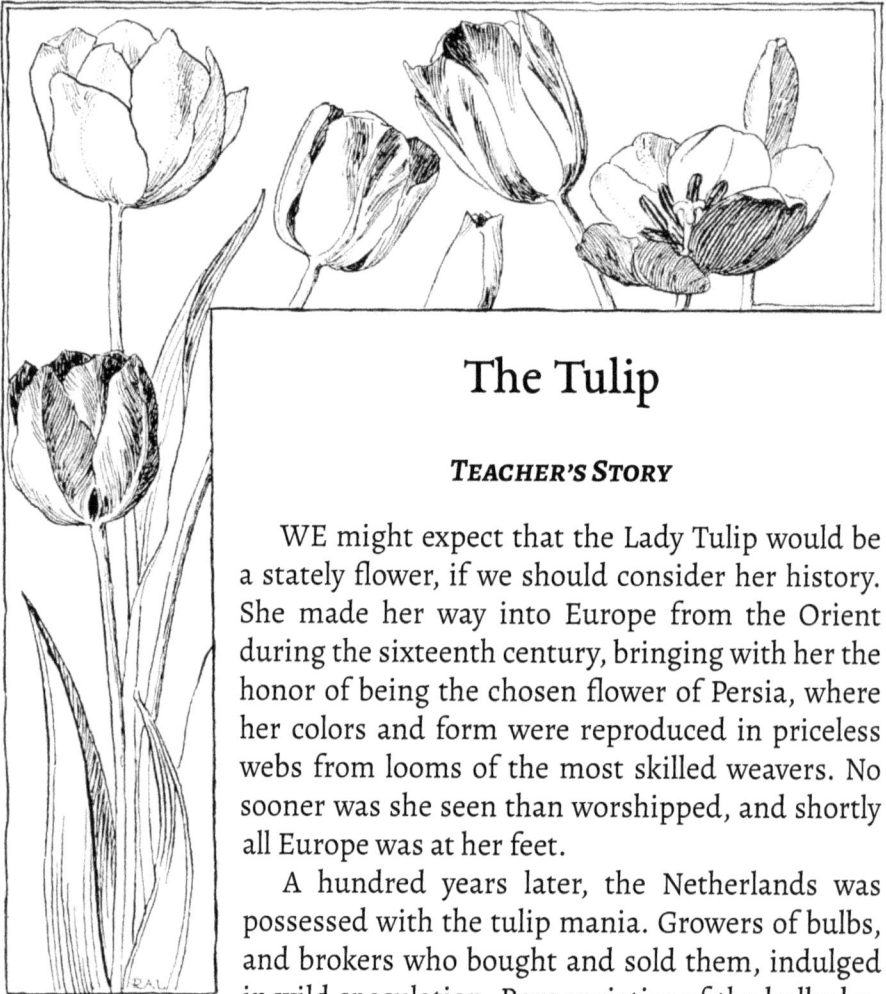

The Tulip

WE might expect that the Lady Tulip would be a stately flower, if we should consider her history. She made her way into Europe from the Orient during the sixteenth century, bringing with her the honor of being the chosen flower of Persia, where her colors and form were reproduced in priceless webs from looms of the most skilled weavers. No sooner was she seen than worshipped, and shortly all Europe was at her feet.

A hundred years later, the Netherlands was possessed with the tulip mania. Growers of bulbs, and brokers who bought and sold them, indulged in wild speculation. Rare varieties of the bulbs became more costly than jewels, one of the famous black tulips being sold for about $1800. Since then, the growing of tulips has been one of the noted industries of the Netherlands, and now the bulbs on our market are imported from Holland.

There are a great many varieties of tulips, and their brilliant colors make our gardens gorgeous in early spring. Although this flower is so prim, yet it bears well close observation. The three petals, or inner segments of the perianth, are more exquisite in texture and in satiny gloss on their inner surface than are the three outer segments or sepals; each petal is like grosgrain silk, the fine ridges uniting at the central thicker portion. In the red varieties, there is a six pointed star at

Tulips come in an abundance of shapes and colors

the heart of the flower, usually yellow or yellow-margined, each point of the star being at the middle of a petal or sepal; the three points on the petals are longer than those on the sepals.

When the flower's bud first appears, it is nestled down in the center of the plant, scarcely above the ground. It is protected by three green sepals. As it stretches up, the bud becomes larger and the green of the sepals takes on the color of the tulip flower, until when it opens there is little on the outside of the sepals to indicate that they once were green. But they still show that they are sepals, for they surround the petals, each standing out and making the flower triangular in shape as we look into it. During storms and dark days, the sepals again partially close about the flower.

The seed-vessel stands up, a stout, three-sided, pale green column at the center of the flower, in some varieties, its three-lobed yellowish stigma making a Doric capital; in others, the divisions are so curled as to make the capital almost Ionian. The six stout, paddle-shaped stamens have their bases expanded so as to encircle completely the base of the pistil column; these wide filaments are narrower just below the point where the large anthers join. The anther opens along each side to discharge the pollen; however, the anthers flare out around the seed vessel and do not reach half way to the stigma, which is probably the tulips' way of inducing the insects to carry their pollen, since the bees cannot reach the nectar at the base of the pistil without dusting themselves with pollen.

The flower stem is stout, pale green, covered with a whitish bloom. The leaves are long, trough-shaped and narrow with parallel veins; the bases of the lower ones encircle the flower stem and have their edges more or less ruffled and their tips recurved; the upper leaves do not completely encircle the flower stem at their bases. The texture of the leaves is somewhat softer on the inside than on the outside, and both sides are grayish green.

After the petals and stamens are dropped the seed-vessel looks like an ornamental tip to the flower stem; it is three-sided, and has within double rows of seeds along each angle. The seeds should not be allowed to ripen as they thus take too much strength from the bulbs.

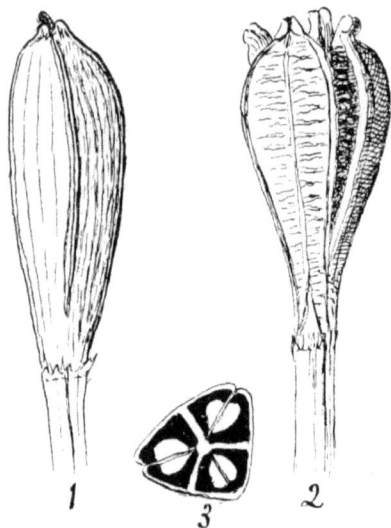

Tulip seed-capsule.
1. Tulip seed-capsule; 2. the same opened; 3. cross section of same.

The bulb is formed of several coats, or layers, each of which extends upwards and may grow into a leaf; this shows that the bulb is made up of leaves which are thickened with the food which is stored up in them during one season, so as to start the plant growing early the next spring. In the heart of each bulb is a flower bud, sheltered and cuddled by the fleshy leaf-layers around it, which protect it during the winter and furnish it food in the spring. This structure of the bulb explains why the leaves clasp the flower stem at their bases. The true roots are below the bulb, making a thick tassel of white rootlets, which reach deep into the soil for food and water.

Tulips are very accommodating; they will grow in almost any soil if it is well drained, so that excessive moisture may not rot the bulbs. In preparing a bed, it should be rounded up so as to shed water; it should also be worked deep and made rich. If the soil is stiff and clayey, set bulbs only three inches deep, with a handful of sand beneath each. If the soil is mellow loam, set the bulbs four inches deep and from four to six inches apart each way, depending on the size of the bulbs. They should be near enough so that when they blossom the bed will be covered and show no gaps. Take care that the pointed tip of the bulb is upward and that it does not fall to one side as it is covered. October is the usual time for planting as the beds are often used for other flowers during the summer. However, September is not too early for the planting, as the more root growth made before the ground freezes, the better; moreover, the early buyers have best choice of bulbs. The beds should be protected by a mulch of straw or leaves during the winter, which should be raked off as soon as the ground is thawed in the spring. The blossoms should be cut as soon as they wither, in order that the new bulbs which form within and at the sides of the parent bulb may have all of the plant food, which would otherwise go to form seed. Tulips may be grown from seed, but it takes from five to seven years to obtain blossoms, which may be quite unlike the parent and worthless, The bulblets grow to a size for blooming in two or three years; the large one which forms in the center of the plant will bloom the next season.

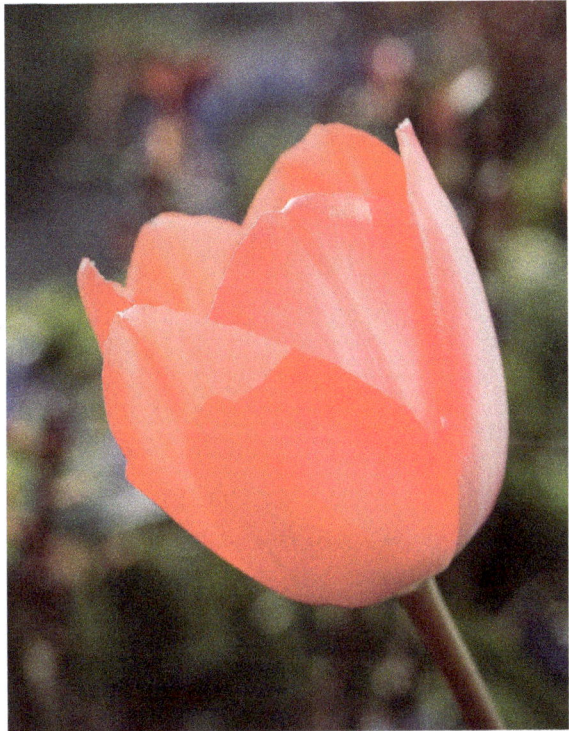

LESSON

Leading thought— The tulips blossom early, because they have food stored in the bulbs the year before, ready to use early in the spring. There are many varieties; each is worth studying carefully, and we should all know how to grow these beautiful flowers.

Methods— These observations may be made upon tulips in school gardens or bouquets. The best methods of cultivating should be a part of the garden training. For this, consult the seed catalogues; also let the pupils form some idea of the number of varieties from the seed catalogues. Water-color drawings should be a large factor in studying the tulip. The red varieties are best for beginning the study, and then follow with the other colors; note differences.

Observations—

1. What is the color of your tulip? Is it all the same color? Is the bottom of the flower different in color? What is the pretty shape of these different colors at the heart of the flower?

2. Look at a tulip just opening. What causes it to appear so triangular? Can you see that the three sepals are placed outside the petals? Is there any difference in color between the sepals and petals on the inside? On the outside? Are the sepals and petals the same in length and shape? Do you know the name given to this arrangement when sepals and petals look alike in color? Are the three petals more satiny on the inside than the sepals? Is the center part of the petal as soft as the edges?

3. When the tulip flower bud first begins to show, where is it? What color are the sepals which cover it? Describe the opening of the flower. Do the green sepals fall off? What becomes of them?

4. In the open flower, where is the seed-pod, and how does it look? How do the anthers surround the seed-pod, or ovary? Describe the

anthers, or pollen-boxes? What color are they? What color is the pollen? Do the anthers reach up to the stigma, or tip of seed-pod? Where is the nectar in tulips? How do the insects become covered with the pollen in reaching it? Do the flowers remain open during dark and stormy days? Why?

5. Describe the tulip stem and the leaves. Do the leaves completely encircle the flower stem at the base? Are their edges ruffled? In the sprouting plant, do these outer basal leaves enfold the leaves which grow higher on the stem? Are the leaves the same color above and below? What shade of green are they?

6. After the petals have dropped, study the seed-pod. Cut it cross-wise and note how many angles it has. How are these angles filled? Should tulips be allowed to ripen seeds? Why not?

7. Study a bulb of a tulip. There are outer and inner layers and a heart. What part of the plant do the outer layers make? What part does the center make? Where are the true roots of the tulip?

8. When should tulip bulbs be planted? How should you prepare the soil? How protect the bed during the winter? How long would it take to grow the flowers from the seed? Where are most of our bulbs grown? Do you know about the history of tulips?

Supplementary reading— Bulbs and Bulb-Culture, Peter Henderson; *Plants and their Children*, Dana, p. 216; *Mary's Garden and How It Grew*, Duncan, Ch. XXVI; *Bulbs and How to Grow Them*, Doubleday-Page Co.

The Pansy

TEACHER'S STORY

SOME people are pansy-faced and some pansies are human-faced, and for some occult reason this puts people and pansies on a distinctly chummy basis. When we analyze the pansy face, we find that the dark spots at the bases of the side petals make the eyes, the lines radiating from them looking quite eyelashy. The opening to the nectar-tube makes the nose, while the spot near the base of the lower petal has to do for a mouth, the nectar guiding-lines being not unlike whiskers. Meanwhile, the two upper petals give a "high-browed" look to the pansy countenance, and make it a wise and knowing little face.

The pansy nectar is hidden in the spur made by the lower petal extending behind the flower. The guiding lines on the lower and side petals all converge, pointing directly to the opening which leads to this nectar-well, telling the secret to every bee that flies. Moreover, the broad lower petal is a platform for the lady bee to alight upon, while she probes the nectar-well with her tongue.

The little pansy-man

But at the door leading to the nectar-well sits a little man; his head is green, he wears a white cape with a scalloped, reddish brown collar, and he sits with his bandy legs pushed back into the spur as if he were taking a foot bath in nectar. This little pansy man has plenty of work to do; for his mouth, which is large and at the top of his green head, is the stigma. The cape is made of five overlapping stamens, the brown, scalloped collar being the anthers; his legs consist of prolongations of the two lower stamens. And when the bee probes the nectar-well with her tongue, she tickles the little man's feet so that his head and shoulders wriggle; and thus she brushes the pollen dust from his collar against her fuzzy face, and at the same time his mouth receives the pollen from her dusty coat.

As the pansy matures, the little man grows still more manlike; after a time he sheds his anther cape, and we can see that his body is the ribbed seed-pod. He did not eat pollen for nothing, for he is full of growing seeds. Sometimes the plush brushes, which are above his head in the pansy flower, become filled with pollen, and perhaps he gets a mouthful of it, although these brushes are supposed to keep out intruders.

The pansy sepals, five in number, are fastened at about one-third of their length, their heart-shaped bases making a little green ruffle around the stem where it joins the flower. There is one sepal above and two at each side, but none below the nectar-spur. The flower stem is quite short and always bends politely so the pansy can look sidewise at us instead of staring straight upward. The plant stem is angled and crooked and stout. In form, the leaves are most capricious; some are long and pointed, others wide and rounded. The edges are slightly

21

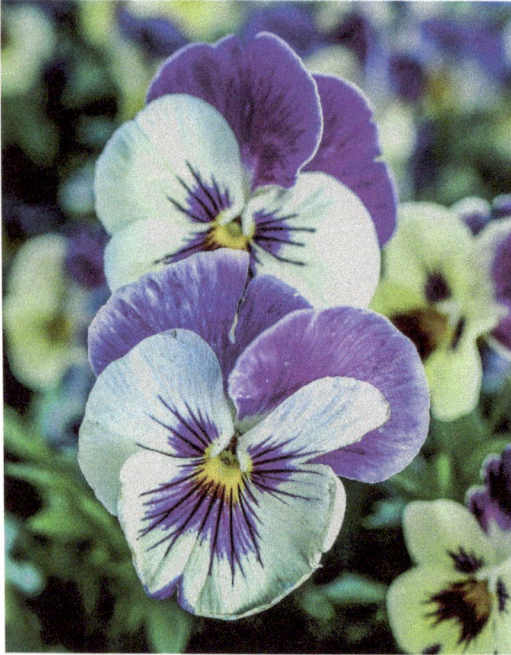

scalloped and the leaf may have at its base a pair of large, deeply lobed stipules. In a whole pansy bed it would be quite impossible to find two leaves just alike.

The pansy ripens many seeds. The ribbed seed-capsule, with its base set comfortably in the faithful sepals, finally opens in three valves and the many seeds are scattered. To send them as far afield as possible, the edges of each valve of the pod curl inward, and snap the seeds out as boys snap apple seeds from the thumb and finger.

Pansies like deep, rich and cool, moist soil. They are best suited to a northern climate, and prefer the shady side of a garden to the full sunshine. The choice varieties are perpetuated through cuttings. They may be stuck in the open ground in summer in a half-shady place and should be well-watered in dry weather. All sorts of pansies are readily raised from seed sown in spring or early summer, and seedlings, when well established, do not suffer, as a rule, from winter frosts.

The general sowing for the production of early spring bloom is made out of doors in August, while seeds sown indoors from February to June will produce plants to flower intermittently during the late summer and fall months. When sowing pansy seed in August, sow the seed broadcast in a seed-bed out of doors, cover very lightly with fine soil or well-rotted manure, and press the seed in with a small board; then mulch the seed-bed with long, strawy horse manure, from which the small particles have been shaken off, to the thickness of one inch, so as to have the soil well and evenly covered. At the end of two weeks the plants will be up. Then remove the straw gradually, a little at a time, selecting a dull day if possible. Keep the bed moist.

If the pansies are allowed to ripen seeds the season of bloom will be short, for when its seeds are scattered the object of the plant's life is accomplished. Besides, the plant has not vitality enough

After flowering, a seed capsule matures, eventually opening as seen here.

to perfect seeds and continue its bloom, and flowers borne with the forming seeds are smaller than the earlier ones. But if the flowers are kept plucked as they open, the plants persistently put forth new buds. The plucked flowers will remain in good condition longer if picked in the early morning before the bees begin paying calls, for a fertilized flower fades more quickly than one which has received no pollen.

LESSON

Leading thought— The pansy is a member of the violet family. The flower often resembles a face; the colors, markings and fragrance all attract the bees, who visit it for the nectar hidden in the spur of the lower petal.

Method— The children naturally love pansies because of the resemblance of these flowers to quaint little faces. They become still more interested after they see the little man with the green head, which appears in the flower as it fades. A more practical interest may be cultivated by studying the great numbers of varieties in the seed catalogs and learning their names. This is one of the studies which leads directly to gardening. There are many beautiful pansy poems which should be read in connection with the lesson.

Observations—

1. How does the pansy flower resemble a face? Where are the eyes? The nose? The mouth? How many petals make the pansy forehead? The cheeks? The chin?

2. Where is the nectar in the pansy? Which petal forms the nectar-tube?

3. Describe how a bee gets the nectar. Where does she stand while probing with her tongue?

4. Where is the pollen in the pansy? What is the peculiar shape of the anthers? How do the two lower stamens differ in form from the three upper ones?

5. Where is the stigma? Does the bee's tongue go over it or under it to reach the nectar? Describe the pansy arrangement for dusting the bee with pollen and for getting pollen from her tongue.

6. Observe the soft little brushes at the base of the two side petals. What do you think they are for?

7. Take a fading flower; remove the petals, and see the little man sitting with his crooked legs in the nectar-tube. What part of the flower makes the man's head? What parts form his cape? Of what is his pointed, scalloped collar formed?

8. How many sepals has the pansy? Describe them. How are they attached? When the flower fades and the petals fall, do the sepals also fall?

9. Where in the flower is the young seed-pod? Describe how this looks after the petals have fallen.

10. Describe how the seed-pod opens. How many seeds are there in it? How are they scattered?

11. Study the pansy stem. Is it solid? Is it smooth or rough? Is it curved? Does it stand up straight or partially recline on the ground?

12. Take a pansy leaf and sketch it with the stipules at its base. Can you find two pansy leaves exactly alike in shape, color and size?

13. At what time should the pansy seed be planted? How should the soil be prepared?

Supplementary reading— "April Fools" (p. 50), "Pansy Song" (p. 125), *Nature in Verse*, compiled by Mary J. Lovejoy; "Garden Folk" (p. 179), "Pansies" pp. 183-184, *Among Flowers and Trees with the Poets*, Wait and Leonard; "A Yellow Pansy" (p. 124), *Nature Pictures by American Poets* compiled by Annie Russell Marble.

I dropped a seed into the earth. It grew, and the plant was mine. It was a wonderful thing, this plant of mine. I did not know its name, and the plant did not bloom. All I know is that I planted something apparently as lifeless as a grain of sand and there came forth a green and living thing unlike the seed, unlike the soil in which it stood, unlike the air into which it grew. No one could tell me why it grew, nor how. It had secrets all its own, secrets that baffle the wisest men; yet this plant was my friend. It faded when I withheld the light, it wilted when I neglected to give it water, it flourished when I supplied its simple needs. One week I went away on a vacation, and when I returned the plant was dead; and I missed it.

Although my little plant had died so soon, it had taught me a lesson; and the lesson is that it is worth while to have a plant.

—THE NATURE-STUDY IDEA, L. H. BAILEY.

Pansy displaying the two upper overlapping petals, the two side petals, and the single bottom petal

The Bleeding Heart

*"The summer's flower is to the summer sweet,
Though to itself it only live and die."*

—SHAKESPEARE.

FOR the intricate structure of this type of flower, the bleeding heart is much more easily studied than its smaller wild sisters, the Dutchman's breeches or squirrel corn; therefore it is well to study these flowers when we find them in profusion in our gardens, and the next spring we may study the wildwood species more understandingly.

The flowers of the bleeding heart are beautiful jewel-like pendants arranged along the stem according to their age; the mature flower, ready to shed its petals, is near the main stem, while the tiny unopened bud is hung at the very tip, where new buds are constantly being formed during a long season of bloom. This flower has a strange modification of its petals; the two pink outer ones, which make the heart, are really little pitchers with nectar at their bottoms, and although they hang mouth downwards the nectar does not flow out. When these outer petals are removed, we can see the inner pair placed opposite to them, the two of them close together and facing each other like two grooved ladles. Just at the mouth of the pitchers these inner petals are almost divided crosswise; and the parts that extend beyond are spoon-shaped, like the bowls of two spoons which have been pinched out so as to make a wide, flat ridge along their centers. These spoon-bowls unite at the tip, and between them they clasp the anthers and stigma. Special attention should be given to the division between the two portions of these inner petals; for it is a hinge, the workings of which are of much importance to the flower. On removing the outer petals, we find a strange framework around which the heart-shaped part of the flower seems to be modeled. These are filaments of the stamens grouped in threes on each side; the two outer ones of each group are widened into frills on the outer edge, while the central one is stiffer and narrower. At the mouth of the pitchers all these filaments unite in a tube around the style; near the stigma they split apart into six short, white, threadlike filaments, each bearing a small, brilliant yellow anther. So close together are these anthers that they are completely covered by the spoon-bowls made by the inner petals, the pollen mass being flat and disklike. During the period when the pollen is produced, the stigma is flat and immature; but after the pollen is shed, it becomes rounded into lobes ready to receive pollen from other flowers.

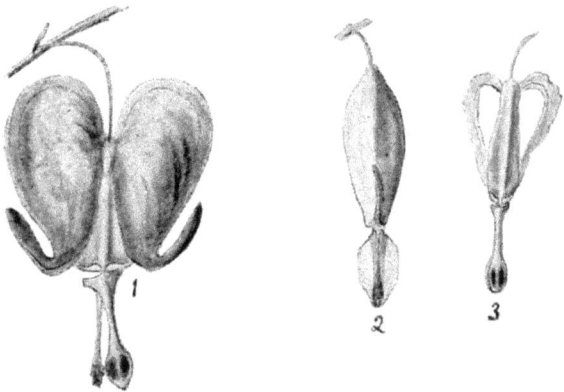

1, Flower of bleeding hear with swing-door ajar. 2, Side-view of flower showing the broad lips of the inner petals. 3, Flower with outer petals removed showing inner petals--and the heart-shaped bases of the stamens.

Although the description of the plant of this flower is most complex and elaborate, the workings of the flower are most simple. As the nectar-pitchers hang mouth down, the bee must cling to the flower while probing upward. In doing this she invariably pushes against the outside of the spoon-bowls, and the hinge at their base allows her to

27

The two inner petals are made visible when the two pink outer petals are pulled apart. Their shape yields the common name "lady-in-a-bath".

push them back while the mass of pollen is thrust against her body; as this hinge works both ways, she receives the pollen first on one side and then on the other, as she probes the nectar-pitchers. And perhaps the next flower she visits may have shed its pollen, and the swing door will uncover the ripe stigma ready to receive the pollen she brings.

The sepals are two little scales opposite the bases of the outer petals. Before the flower opens, the "spouts of the nectar-pitchers" are clamped up on either side of the spoon-bowls, as if to keep everything safe until the right moment comes; at first they simply spread apart, but later curve backward. The seed-pod is long and narrow, and in cross-section is seen to contain two compartments with seeds growing on every side of the partition.

The bleeding heart is a native of China, and was introduced into Europe about the middle of the last century.

Reference— Our Garden Flowers, Keeler.

LESSON

Leading thought— The bleeding heart flower has its pollen and stigma covered by a double swing door, which the bees push back and forth when they gather the nectar.

Method— Bring a bouquet of the bleeding heart to the schoolroom, and let each pupil have a stem with its flowers in all stages. From this study, encourage them to watch these flowers when the insects are visiting them.

Observations—

1. How are these flowers supported? Do they open upward or downward? Can you see the tiny sepals?

2. How many petals can you see in this flower? What is the shape of the two outer petals? How do they open? Where is the nectar developed in these petals?

3. Take off the two outer petals and study the two inner ones. What is their shape near the base? How are their parts shaped which project beyond the outer petals? What does the spoon-end of these petals cover? Can you find the hinge in these petals?

4. Where are the stamens? How many are there? Describe the shape of the stamens near the base. How are they united at the tip?

5. Where is the stigma? The style? The ovary?

6. Supposing a bee is after the nectar, where must she rest while probing for it? Can she get the nectar without pushing against the flat projecting portion of the inner petals? When she pushes these spoon-bowls back, what happens? Does she get dusted with pollen? After she leaves, does the door swing back? Suppose she visits another flower which has shed its pollen, will she carry pollen to its stigma? Does she have to work the hinged door to do this?

The Poppies

TEACHER'S STORY

PERHAPS we might expect that a plant which gives strange dreams to those who eat of its juices should not be what it seems in appearance. I know of nothing so deceptive as the appearance of the poppy buds, which, rough and hairy, droop so naturally that it seems as if their weight must compel the stem to bend; and yet, if we test it, we find the stem is as stiff as if made of steel wire. Moreover, the flower and the ripened seed-capsule must be far heavier than the bud; and yet, as soon as the flower is ready to open, the stem straightens up, although it does not always remove the traces of the crook; and after the capsule is full of ripened seed, the stem holds it up particularly stiff, as if inviting the wind to shake out the seeds.

The rough covering of the bud consists of two sepals, as can be easily seen; but if we wish to see the poppy shed its sepals, we must get up in the morning, for the deed is usually done as soon as the first rays of the early sun bring their message of a fair day. The sepals break off at their base and fall to the ground. The two opposite outer petals unfold, leaving the two inner petals standing erect and on guard about the precious pollen, until the sunshine folds them back. An open poppy, when looked at below, shows two petals, each semicircular, and overlapping each other slightly; looked at from above, we see two petals, also half circles, set at right angles to the lower two, and divided from each other by the pistil.

The pistil of the poppy is, from the beginning, a fascinating box. At

first, it is a vase with a round, circular cover, upon which are ridges, placed like the spokes of a wheel. If these ridges are looked at with a lens, particles of pollen may be seen adhering to them; this fact reveals the secret that each ridge is a stigma, and all of these radiating stigmas are joined so as better to catch the pollen. In a circle of fringe

The poppy seed-shaker

about the pistil are the stamens. In the study of the stamens, we should note whether their filaments expand or dilate near the anthers, and we should also note the color of the masses of pollen which crowd out from the anthers.

Despite the many varieties of poppies, there are only four species commonly cultivated. The opium poppy has upon its foliage a white bloom, the filaments of its stamens are dilated at the top, and its seed-capsule is smooth. The oriental poppy has all of these characters, except that its foliage is green and not covered with bloom. Its blossom is scarlet and very large and has a purple center in the petals and purple stamens; it has

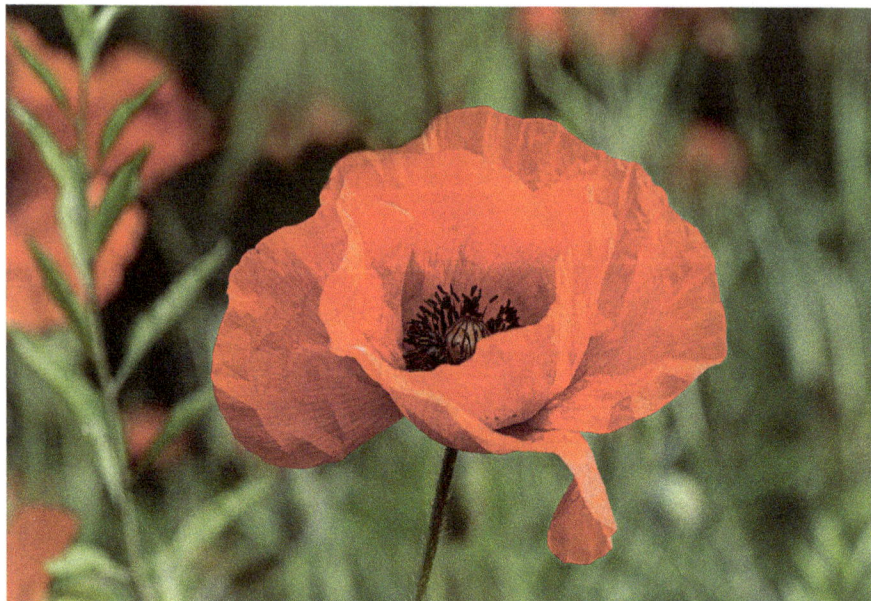

Oriental poppy

three sepals. Its flower stalks are stout and leafy. The corn poppy, which grows in the fields of Europe, is a weed we gladly cultivate. This, naturally, has red petals and is dark at the center of the flower; but it has been changed by breeding until now we have many varieties. Its foliage is finely cut and very bristly or hairy. Its seed-capsule is not bristly. To see this poppy at its best, we should visit northern Italy or southern France in late May, where it makes the grain fields gorgeous. This is the original parent of all the Shirley poppies. The Arctic, or Iceland poppy, has flowers of satiny texture and finely crumpled; its colors are yellow, orange or white, but never scarlet like the corn poppy; it has no leaves on its flower stem, and its seed-capsule is hairy. Of these four species, the opium poppy and the corn poppy are annuals, while the Arctic and the Oriental species are perennials.

The bees are over-fond of the poppy pollen and it is a delight to watch the fervor with which they simply wallow in it, brushing off all of the grains possible onto their hairy bodies. I have often seen a honey-bee seize a bunch of the anthers and rub them against the under side of her body, meanwhile standing on her head in an attitude of delirious joy. As showing the honey-bee's eye for color, I have several times seen a bee drop to the ground to examine a red petal which had fallen. This was plain evidence that she trusted to the color to guide her to the pollen.

But perhaps it is the development of the poppy seed-capsule which we find the most interesting of the poppy performances. After fertilization, the stigma-disk develops a scalloped edge, a stigma rounding out the point of each scallop; and a sharp ridge, which continues the length of the globular capsule, runs from the center of each scallop. If examined on the inside, it will be seen

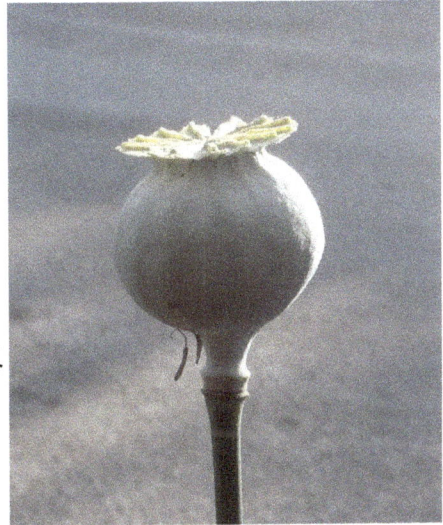

Oriental poppy seed shaker

that the ridge on the capsule is the edge of a partition which extends only part way toward the center of the capsule. On these partitions, the little seeds are grown in great profusion, and when they ripen, they fall together in the hollow center of the seed-box. But how are they to get out? This is a point of interest for the children to observe, and they should watch the whole process. Just beneath the stigma-disk, and between each two of the sharp ridges, the point loosens; later, it turns outward and back, leaving a hole which leads directly into the central hollow portion of the capsule. The way these points open is as pretty a story as I know in flower history. This beautiful globular capsule, with its graceful pedestal where it joins the stem, is a seed-shaker instead of a salt or pepper-shaker. Passing people and animals push against it and the stiff stem bends and then springs back, sending a little shower of seeds this way and that; or a wind sways the stalk, and the seeds are sown, a few at a time, and in different conditions of season and weather. Thus, although the poppy puts all her eggs in one basket, she sends them to market a few at a time. The poppy seed is a pretty object, as seen through the lens. It is shaped like a round bean, and is covered with a honey comb network.

LESSON

Leading thought— The poppies shed their sepals when the flowers expand; they offer quantities of pollen to the bees, which are very fond of it. The seed-capsule develops holes around the top, through which the seeds are shaken, a few at a time.

Method— It is best to study these flowers in the garden, but the lesson may be given if some of the plants with the buds are brought to the schoolroom, care being taken that they do not droop. If the teacher thinks wise, the pupils might prepare an English theme on the subject of the opium poppy and the terrible effects of opium upon the eastern nations.

Observations—

1. Look at the bud of the poppy; how is it covered? How many sepals? Can you see where they unite? Is the stem bent because the bud is heavy? What happens to this crook in the stem when the flower opens? Does the crook always straighten out completely?

2. Describe how the poppy sheds its sepals. At what time of day do the poppies usually open?

3. Look at the back of, or beneath, an open flower. How many petals do you see? How are they arranged? Look at the base of the flower. How many petals do you see? How are they arranged in relation to the lower petals and to the pistil?

4. Look at the globular pistil. Describe the disk which covers it. How many ridges on this disk? How are they arranged? Look at the ridges with a lens and tell what they are.

5. Look at the stamens. How are they arranged? Describe the anthers—their color, and the color of the pollen. Watch the bees working on the poppies, and note if they are after nectar or pollen.

6. Find all the varieties of poppies possible, and note the colors of the petals on the outside, the inside and at the base; of the stamens, including filaments, anthers and pollen; of the pistil-disk and ovary. Sketch the poppy opened, and also in the bud. Sketch a petal, a stamen and the pistil, in separate studies.

7. Study the poppy seed-box as it ripens. How does the stigma-disk look? What is the shape of the capsule below the disk? Is it ridged? What relation do its ridges bear to the stigma ridges on the disk? Cut

A poppy preparing to bloom

a capsule open, and note what these ridges on the outside have to do with the partitions inside. Where are the seeds borne?

8. Note the development of the holes beneath the edge of the disk of the poppy capsule. How are they made? What are they for? How are the seeds shaken from these holes? What shakes the poppy seed-box and helps sow the seeds? Look at a seed through a lens, and describe its form and decoration.

9. Notice the form of the poppy leaf, and note whether it is hairy or covered with bloom. What is there peculiar about the smell of the poppy plant? Where do poppies grow wild?

10. Is the slender stem smooth or grooved and hairy? Is it solid or hollow?

11. When a stem or leaf is pierced or broken off, what is the color of the juice which exudes? Does this juice taste sweet or bitter and unpleasant? Do you know what harmful drug is manufactured from the juice of one species of poppy? What countries cultivate and use it most extensively?

The California Poppy

LTHOUGH this brilliant flower blossoms cheerfully for us in our Eastern gardens, we can never understand its beauty until we see it glowing in masses on the California foothills. We can easily understand why it was selected as the flower of that great State, since it burnished with gold the hills, above the gold buried below; and in that land that prides itself upon its sunshine, these poppies seem to shine up as the sun shines down. The literature of California, and it has a noble literature of its own, is rich in tributes to this favored flower. There is a peculiar beauty in the contrast between the shining flower and its pale blue-green, delicate masses of foliage. Although it is called a poppy and belongs to the poppy family, yet it is not a true poppy, but belongs to a genus named after a German who visited California early in the nineteenth century, accompanying a Russian scientific expedition; this German's name was Eschscholtz, and he, like all visitors, fell in love with this brilliant flower, and in his honor it was named Eschscholtzia (es-sholts-ia) californica. This is not nearly so pretty, nor so descriptive, as the name given to this poppy by the Spanish settlers on the Pacific Coast, for they called it *Copa-de-oro*, cups of gold.

The bud of the Eschscholtzia is a pretty thing; it stands erect on the slender, rather long stem, which flares near the bud to an urnlike pedestal with a slightly ruffled rim, on which the bud is set. This rim is often pink above, and remains as a pretty base for the seed-pod. But in some garden varieties, the rim is lacking. The bud itself is covered with a peaked cap, like a Brownie's toboggan cap stuffed full to the tip. It is the shape of an old-fashioned candle extinguisher; it is pale green, somewhat ribbed, and has a rosy tip; it consists of two sepals, which have been sewed together by Mother Nature so skillfully that we cannot see the seams. One of the most interesting performances

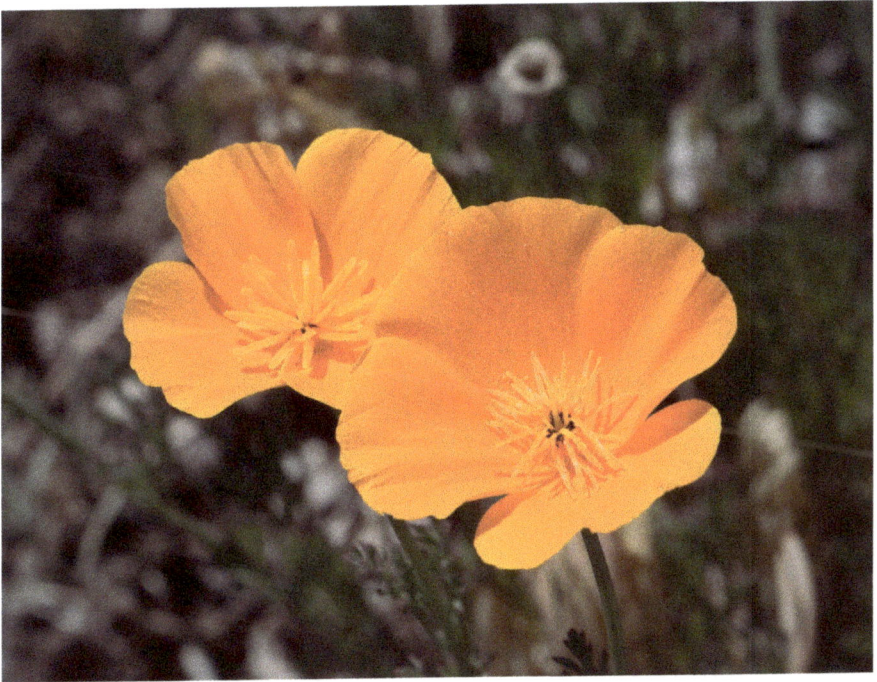

to watch that I know, is the way this poppy takes off its cap before it bows to the world. Like magic the cap loosens around the base; it is then pushed off by the swelling expanding petals until completely loosened, and finally it drops.

The petals are folded under the cap in an interesting manner. The outer petal enfolds all the others as closely as it can, and its mate within it enfolds the other two, and the inner two enfold the stamens with their precious gold dust. When only partially opened, the petals cling protectingly about the many long stamens; but when completely opened, the four petals flare wide, making a flower with a golden rim and orange center, although among our cultivated varieties they range from orange to an anaemic white. To one who loves them in their glorious native hues, the white varieties seem almost repulsive. Compare one of these small, pale flowers with the great, rich, orange ones that glorify some favored regions in the Mojave Desert, and we feel the enervating and decadent influence of civilization.

The anthers are many and long, and are likely to have a black dot on the short filament; at first, the anthers stand in a close cluster at the center of the flower, but later they flare out in a many pointed star. Often, when the flowers first open, especially the earlier ones, the stigmas cannot be seen at all; but after a time the three, or even six stigmas, spread wide athwart the flower and above the stamen-star, where they may receive pollen from the visiting insects. The anthers give abundance of pollen, but there is said to be no nectary present. This flower is a good guardian of its pollen, for it closes during the nights and also on dark and rainy days, only exposing its riches when the sunshine insures insect visitors. It closes its

California Poppy

petals in the same order in which they were opened in our Eastern gardens, although there are statements that in California, each petal folds singly around its own quota of anthers. The insects in California take advantage of the closing petals and often get a night's lodging within them, where they are cozily housed with plenty of pollen for supper and breakfast; and they pay their bill in a strange way by carrying off as much of the golden meal as adheres to them, just as the man who weighs gold-dust gets his pay from what adheres to the pan of his scales.

After the petals fall, the little pod is very small, but its growth is as astonishing as that of Jack's beanstalk; it finally attains a slim length of three inches, and often more. It is grooved, the groove running

Californian Poppies, at the Antelope Valley California Poppy Reserve

straight from its rimmed base to its rosy tip; but later a strange twisting takes place. If we open one of these capsules lengthwise, we must admire the orderly way in which the little green seeds are fastened by delicate white threads, in two crowded rows, the whole length of the pod.

The leaf is delicately cut and makes the foliage a fine mass, but each leaf is quite regular in its form. It has a long, flattened petiole, which broadens and clasps the stem somewhat at its base. Its blade has five main divisions, each of which is deeply cut into fingerlike lobes. The color of this foliage and its form show adaptations to desert conditions.

This plant has a long, smooth tap root, especially adapted for storing food and moisture needed during the long, dry California summers; for it is perennial in its native state, although in the wintry East, we plant it as an annual.

LESSON

Leading thought— The California poppy is a native of California. It blossoms during the months of February, March and April in greatest abundance. It is found in the desert as well as among the foothills.

Method— If possible, the students should study this in the garden. In the East, it flowers until frost comes, and affords a delightful subject for a September lesson. In California it should be studied in the spring, when the hills are covered with them. But the plant may be brought into the schoolroom, root and all, and placed in a jar, under which conditions it will continue to blossom.

Observations—

1. Look at the California poppy as a whole and tell, if you can, why it is so beautiful when in blossom.

'Purple Gleam', a genetic variation of the california poppy

2. Look at the flower bud. What sort of a stem has it? What is the shape of the stem just below the bud? What is the color of the little rim on which the bud rests? What peculiarity has this bud? Describe the little cap.

3. Watch a flower unfold. What happens to the "toboggan cap?" How does the bud look after the cap is gone? What is its appearance when the petals first open? When they are completely open?

4. Describe the anthers. How do they stand when the flower first opens? How later? Can you see the stigmas at first? Describe them as they look later.

5. Does the poppy remain open at night? Does it remain open during cloudy or rainy weather? Why?

6. Do the petals have the same position that they did in the bud? As the flower matures, note how each petal curls. Do they all fall at once? Are there any anthers left after the petals fall?

7. How does the little pod look when the petals first fall? What happens to it later? Note the little rim at its base. Cut the seed-pod open lengthwise, examine the seeds with a lens, and describe how they are fastened to the sides of the pod. Are the ribs straight from end to end in the pod at first? Do they remain in this position? How does the pod open and scatter its seeds?

8. Study the leaf of this California poppy. Describe how it joins the stem. Sketch a leaf showing its chief divisions into leaflets and how each leaflet is divided. Note that the juice of the stem has the peculiar odor of muriatic acid.

9. Look at the root. Do you think it is fitted to sustain the plant through a long, dry summer? What kind of summers do they have in California? Where does the poppy grow wild?

10. Read all the accounts you can find of the California poppy, and write a little theme describing why it was chosen as the flower of that great State, and how it came by its name.

> *In a low brown meadow on a day*
> *Down by the autumn sea,*
> *I saw a flash of sudden light*
> *In a sweep of lonely gray;*
> *As if a star in a clouded night*
> *One moment had looked on me*
> *And then withdrawn; as if the spring*
> *Had sent an oriole back to sing*
> *A silent song in color, where*
> *Other silence was too hard to bear.*
> *I found it and left it in its place,*
> *The sun-born flower in cloth of gold*
> *That April owns, but cannot hold*
> *From spending its glory and its grace*
> *On months that always love it less,*
> *But take its splendid alms in their distress.*
> *Back I went through the gray and the brown,*
> *Through the weed-woven trail to the distant town;*
> *The flower went with me, fairly wrought*
> *Into the finest fiber of my thought.*
> —A CALIFORNIA POPPY IN NOVEMBER, IRENE HARDY.

The Nasturtium

TEACHER'S STORY

"Little warriors, brave and fearless, with shields of emerald green,
Are climbing over fence rails, and everywhere are seen
Looking down on every side, while her brave Nasturtium army,
Queen Nature views with pride."

—RAY LAURANCE.

It is quite fitting that the nasturtium leaves should be shaped like shields, for that is one of their uses; they are shields to protect the young nasturtium seeds from the hot sun and from the view of devouring enemies. The nasturtiums are natives of Peru and Chili, and it is fitting that the leaves should develop in shield-shape, and the shields overlap until they form a tent to shade the tender developing fruit from the burning sun. But they were never meant to shield the flower, which thrusts its brilliant petals out between the shields, and calls loudly to the world to admire it. It would indeed be a pity for such a remarkable flower to remain hidden; its five sepals are united at their base, and the posterior one is extended into a long spur, a tube with a delectable nectar-well at its tip. The five petals are set around the mouth of this tube, the two upper ones differing in appearance

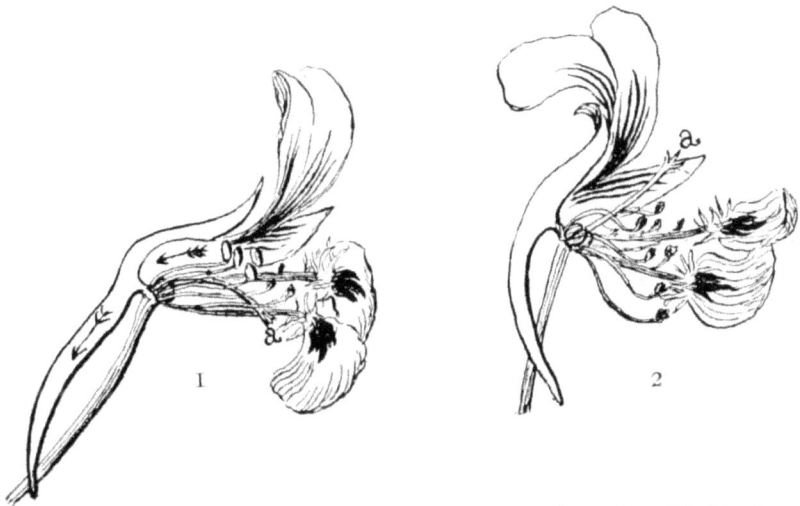

1. *Nasturtium flower in early stage of blossoming. Note the anthers lifted in the path to the nectar which is indicated by the arrow. The closed stigma is shown deflected at a.*

2. *The same flower in later stage; the anthers are empty and deflected. The stigma is raised (a) in the nectar path.*

and office from those below; these two stand up like a pair of fans, and on them are lines which converge; on the upper sepals are similar lines pointing toward the same interesting spot. And what do all these lines lead to, except a veritable treasure-cave filled with nectar! The lower petals tell another story; they stand out, making a platform, or doorstep, on which the visiting bee alights. But it requires a big insect to do the work of this flower, and what if some inefficient little bee or fly should alight on the petal-doorstep and steal into the cave surreptitiously! This contingency is guarded against thus: Each of these lower petals narrows to a mere insect footbridge at their inner end; and in order to render this footbridge quite impassable, it is beset with irregular little spikes and projecting fringes, sufficient to perplex or discourage any small insect from crawling that way.

But why all these guiding lines and guarded bridges? If you watch the same blossom for several successive days, it will reveal this secret. When a flower first opens, the stamens are all bent downward, but when an anther is ready to open its pollen doors, the filament lifts it up and places it like a sentinel blocking the doorway to the nectar treasure. Then when the robber comes, whether it be butterfly, bee or hummingbird, it gets a round of pollen ammunition for its dar-

What parts of the flower can you identify in this nasturtium

ing. Perhaps there may be two or three anthers standing guard at the same time, but, as soon as their pollen is exhausted, they shrivel and give room for fresh anthers. Meanwhile, the stigma has its three lobes closed and lying idly behind and below the anthers; after all the pollen is shed, the style raises and takes its position at the cave entrance and opens up its stigmas, like a three-tined fork, to rake the pollen from any visiting insect, thus robbing the robber of precious gold-dust which shall fertilize the seeds in its three-lobed ovary. Although the flower needs to flare its colors wide to call the bees and humming-birds, yet the growing seeds must be protected; therefore, the stem which held the flower up straight, now twists around in a spiral and draws the triplet seeds down behind the green shields.

Nasturtium leaves are very pretty, and are often used as subjects for decorative water-color drawings. The almost circular leaf has its stem attached below and a little at one side of the center; the leaves are brilliant green above but quite pale beneath, and are silvery when placed beneath the water. The succulent stems have a way of twisting half around the wires of the trellis and thus holding the plant secure to its support. But if there is no trellis, the main stem seems to awaken to the responsibility and grows quite stocky, often lifting the plant a foot or two in height, and from its summit sending out a fountain of leaf and flower stems.

The nasturtium is among the most interesting and beautiful of our garden flowers, and will thrive in any warm, sunny, fairly moist place. Its combinations of color are exceedingly rich and brilliant. H. H. says of it:

> "How carelessly it wears the velvet of the same
> Unfathomed red, which ceased when Titian ceased
> To paint it in the robes of doge and priest."

LESSON

Leading thought— The nasturtium has a special arrangement by which it sends its own pollen to other flowers and receives pollen from other flowers by insect messengers.

Method— The nasturtiums and their foliage should be brought into the schoolroom in sufficient quantity so that each child may have a leaf and a flower for study. The object of the lesson is to interest the pupils in studying, in their gardens, one flower from the bud until the petals wither, taking note of what happens each day and keeping a list of the insect visitors.

Observations—

1. Look at the back of the flower. What is there peculiar about the sepals? How many sepals are there? How many join to make the spur? What is in this spur? Taste of the tip. Find where the nectar is.

2. Look the flower in the face. How do the two upper petals differ in shape from the three lower ones? What markings are there on the upper petals? Where do these lines point? Are there any markings on the

sepals pointing in the same direction? If an insect visiting a flower should follow these lines, where would it go?

3. Describe the shape of the lower petals. Suppose a little ant were on one of these petals and she tried to pass over to the nectar-tube or spur, would the fringes hinder her?

4. Look down the throat of the spur, and tell what a bee or other insect would have to crawl over before it could get at the nectar.

5. In your garden, or in the bouquet in the window if you cannot visit a garden, select a nasturtium that is just opening and watch it every day, making the following notes: When the blossom first opens where are the eight stamens? Are the unripe, closed anthers lifted so as to be in the path of the bee which is gathering nectar? How do the anthers open? How is the pollen held up in the path to the nectar? Can you see the stigma of this flower? Where is it? *Note the same flower on successive days:* How many anthers are open and shedding pollen to-day? Are they all in the same position as yesterday? What happens to the anthers which have shed their pollen?

Nasturtium leaf showing the work of serpentine miners

6. When the stigma rises in the nectar path, how does it look? Where are all the anthers when the stigma raises its three tines to rake the pollen off the visiting insect? Do you know why it is an advantage to the nasturtium to develop its seed by the aid of the pollen from another plant?

7. Can you see the beginning of the seed-case when the stigma arises to receive the pollen?

8. The flowers project beyond the leaves. Do the ripening seed-cases do this? What happens to their stems to withdraw them behind the leaf?

9. Sketch a nasturtium leaf, and explain why it is like a shield. How does the leaf look when under water?

10. What sort of stem has the nasturtium? How does it manage to climb the trellis? If it has no trellis to climb, does it lie flat upon the ground?

Some shades of larkspur

The Bee-Larkspur

TEACHER'S STORY

This common flower of our gardens, sending up from a mass of dark, deeply-cut leaves tall racemes of purple or blue flowers, has a very interesting story to tell those who watch it day by day and get acquainted with it and its insect guests. The brilliant color of the flowers is due to the sepals, which are purple or blue, in varying shades; but as if to show that they are sepals instead of petals, each has on the back side near its tip, a green thickened spot. If we glance up the flower stalk, we can see that, in the upper buds, the sepals are green, but in the lower buds they begin to show the blue color; and in a bud just ready to open, we can see that the blue sepals are each tipped with a green knob, and this remains green after the sepals expand. The upper and rearmost sepal is prolonged into a spur, which forms the outside covering of the nectar-spur; it is greenish and wrinkled like a long-wristed, suede glove; two sepals spread wide at the sides and two more below. All this expanse of blue sepals is simply for a background for the petals, which, by their contrasting color, show the bees where to probe for nectar. Such inconsequential petals as they are! Two of them "hold hands" to make an arch over the entrance to the nectar tube; and just below these on each side are two more tiny, fuzzy, spreading petals, often notched at the tip and always hinged in a peculiar way about the upper petal; they stand guard at the door to the nectar storehouse. If we peel off the wrinkled sepal-covering of the spur, we can see the upper petals extending back into it, making a somewhat double-barreled nectary.

If we look into a larkspur flower just opened, we see below the petals a bunch of green anthers, hanging by white threadlike filaments to the center of the flower and looking like a bunch of lilliputian bananas. Behind these anthers is an undeveloped stigma, not visible as yet. After the flower has been open for a short time, three or four of the anthers rise up and stand within the lower petals; while in this position, their white pollen bursts from them, and no bee may then thrust her tongue into the nectar-spur without being powdered with pollen. As soon as the anthers have discharged their pollen, they shrivel and their places are taken by fresh ones. It may require two or three days for all the anthers to lift up and get rid of their pollen. After this has been accomplished, the three white, closely adhering pistils lift up their three stigmas in the self-same path to the nectar; and now they are ready to receive the pollen which the blundering bee brings from other flowers. Since we cannot always study the same flower for several consecutive days, we can read the whole story by studying the flowers freshly opened on the upper portion of the stalk, and those below them that are in more advanced stages.

The bees, especially the bumblebee, will tell the pollenation story to us in the garden. The contrasting color of the petals and sepals tells her where to alight; this she does accurately, and the inconsequential lower petals seem made for her to grasp; she presses them to her breast

1. Drawing of the bee-larkspur flower enlarged
2. The seed capsule of the bee-larkspur

48

with her front and middle legs with a dramatic, almost ecstatic, gesture that is comical to witness, and holds them firmly while she thrusts her head into the opening between them; she probes the spur twice, evidently finding there the two nectar-wells. It is a fascinating pastime to follow her as she goes from flower to flower like a Madam Pompadour, powdered with her white pollen. In order that a bee may work on these flowers, it is necessary that they hang vertically. The tips of the tall flower stalks are likely to bend or curl over; but no matter what direction the broken or bent stem takes, the flowers will twist around on their pedicels until they face the world and the bee, exactly as if they were on a normally erect stem.

All the larkspurs have essentially the same pollen story, although some have only two petals; in every case the anthers at first hang down, and later rise up in the path to the nectar, in order to discharge their pollen; after they wither, the stigmas arise in a similar position.

The bee-larkspur has a very beautiful fruit. It consists of three graceful capsules rising from the same base and flaring out into pointed tips. The seeds are fastened to the curved side of each capsule, which, when ripe, opens so that they may be shaken out by the winds. When studying the bud, we notice two little bracts set at its base and these remain with the fruit.

LESSON

Leading thought— The bee-larkspur begins blossoming early in the season, the blossom stalk elongating and developing new buds at its tip until late in autumn. The flower has a very interesting way of mak-

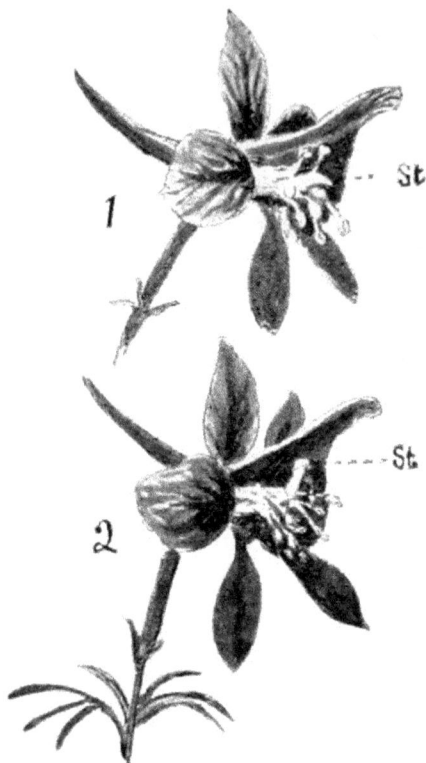

The larkspur
1. showing early stage with stigma deflected.
2. showing advanced stage with stigma raised.

ing the bees carry its pollen.

Method— Bring to the schoolroom a flower stalk of the bee-larkspur, and there study the structure and mechanism of the flower. This lesson should inspire the pupils to observe for themselves the visiting bees and the maturing seeds. Ask them to write an account of a bumblebee making morning calls on the larkspurs.

Observations—

1. Which flowers of the larkspur open first—those near the tip of the stem or those below?

2. Examine the buds toward the tip of the flower stalk. What color are the sepals in these buds? Do the sepals change color as the flower opens? Note the little green knobs which tip the closed sepals that clasp the bud. What color are the sepals on the open flower? Is there any green upon them when open?

3. Where is the nectar-spur? Which sepal forms this? How are the other sepals arranged?

4. Now that we know the flower gets its brilliant color from its sepals, let us find the petals. Look straight into the flower, and note what forms the contrasting color of the heart of the flower; these are the petals. Can you see that two are joined above the opening into the nectar-tube? How many guard the entrance from below? How are these lower petals hinged about the upper one? Peel a sepal-cover from the nectar-spur, and see if the upper petals extend back within the spur, forming nectar-tubes?

5. Take a flower just opened, and describe what you see below the

petals. What is the color of the anthers? Of the filaments? Can you see the stigma?

6. Take a flower farther down the stalk, which has therefore been open longer, and describe the position of the anthers in this. Are there any of them standing upright? Are they discharging their pollen? What color is the pollen? Are these upright anthers in the way of the bee, when she thrusts her tongue into the nectar-tube?

7. Take the oldest flower you can find. What has happened to the anthers? Can you see the pistils in this? In what position now are the stigmas?

8. Push aside the anthers in a freshly opened flower and see if you can find the stigmas. What is their position? How do they change in form and position after the pollen is shed? Do they arise in the path of the bee before all the pollen from the anthers of their own flower is shed? If so, how are they pollenated?

9. *Suggestions for Observation in the Garden*— Watch a bumblebee working on the larkspur and answer the following questions: How does she hold on to the flower? Where does she thrust her tongue? Can she get the nectar without brushing the pollen from the anthers which are lifting up at the opening of the nectar-tube? In probing the older flowers, how would she come in contact with the lifted stigmas? How do the petals contrast in color with the sepals? Does this tell the bees where to look for nectar? Compare the common larkspur with the bee-larkspur, and notice the likeness and difference. What kind of fruit capsules has the bee-larkspur? Describe the seeds, and how they are scattered.

The fleur-de-lis is the national flower of France

The Blue Flag, or Iris

TEACHER'S STORY

Beautiful lily, dwelling by still rivers
   Or solitary mere,
Or where the sluggish meadow brook delivers
   Its waters to the weir!

The burnished dragon fly is thine attendant,
   And tilts against the field,
And down the listed sunbeams rides resplendent
   With steel-blue mail and shield.
     —FROM "FLOWER-DE-LUCE," HENRY W. LONGFELLOW.

The iris blossom has a strange appearance, and this is because nothing in it is as it seems. The style of the pistil is divided into three broad branches and they look like petals; and they have formed a conspiracy with the sepals to make a tunnel for bees, leaving the petals out of the plan entirely and the sepals "rise to the occasion." The petals stand up lonely between the three strangely matched pairs, and all they ac-complish by their purple guiding lines, is to basely deceive the butterflies and other insects which are in the habit of looking for nectar at the center of a flower. If we look directly down into the flower of the blue flag, there are ridges on the broad styles and purple veins on the petals, all pointing plainly to the center of the flower, and any insect alighting there would naturally seek for nectar-wells where all these lines so plainly lead. But there is an "April fool" for the insects which trust to these guides, for there is no nectar to be had there. Dr. Needham, in his admirable study of this flower and its visitors (American Naturalist, May, 1900), tells us that he has seen the little butterflies called "skippers," the flag weevils and the flower beetles all made victims of this deceptive appearance; this is evidence that the nectar guiding lines on flowers are noted and followed by insects.

The blue flag is made for bees; the butterflies and beetles are interlopers and thieves at best. The bees are never deceived into seeking the nectar in the wrong place. They know to a certainty that the sepal with its purple and yellow tip and many guiding lines, although far from the center of the flower, is the sure path to the nectar. A bee alights on the lip of the sepal, presses forward scraping her back against the down-hanging stigma, then scrapes along the open anther which lies along the roof of the tunnel; and she here finds a pair of guiding lines each leading to a nectar-well at the very base of the sepal. The bees which Dr. Needham found doing the greatest work as pollen-carri-

ers were small solitary bees (*Clisodon terminalis* and *Osmia destructa*); each of these alighted with precision on the threshold of the side door, pushed its way in, got the nectar from both wells, came out and sought another side door speedily. One might ask why the bee in coming out did not deposit the pollen from its own anther upon the stigma; but the stigma avoids this by hanging down, like a flap to a tent, above the entrance, and its surface for receiving pollen is directed so that it gathers pollen from the entering bee and turns its back to the bee that is just making its exit.

The arrangement of the flower parts of the iris may be described briefly thus: three petals, three sepals, a style with three branches; the latter being broad and flat and covering the bases of the three sepals, making tubes which lead to the nectar; three anthers lie along the under side of the styles. The wild yellow iris is especially fitted for welcoming the bumblebee as a pollen-carrier, since the door between the style and the sepal is large enough to admit this larger insect. The bumblebees and the honey-bees work in the different varieties of iris in gardens.

In some varieties of iris there is a plush rug along the vestibule floor over which the bee passes to get the nectar. Through a lens, this plush is exquisite—the nap of white filaments standing up and tipped

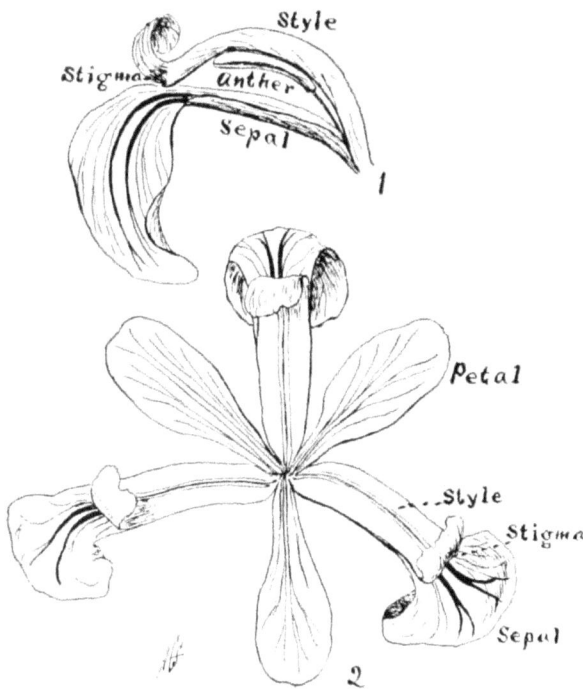

Detail of the blossoms of the blue flag flower.
1. Side-view of the passage to the nectar.
2. Looking directly into the iris flowers. Note the deceiving guide-lines in the petals.

with brilliant yellow. Various theories as to the use of this plush have been advanced, the most plausible being that it is to keep the ants out; but the ant could easily pass along either side of it. While holding an iris in my hand, one day in the garden, a bumblebee visited it eagerly, never noting me; after she had probed the nectar-wells, she probed or nibbled among the plush, working it thoroughly on her way out. Was she a foolish bee, or did she find something there to eat? What child will find if other bees do this?

LESSON

Leading thought— Each iris flower has three side doors leading to the nectar-wells; and the bees, in order to get the nectar, must brush off the pollen dust on their backs.

Method— While the blue flag is the most interesting of our wild species of iris, yet the flower-de-luce, or the garden iris, is quite as valuable for this lesson. The form of the flowers may be studied in the schoolroom, but the pupils should watch the visiting insects in the garden or field.

A white iris

Observations—

1. Look for the side doors of the iris blossom. Which part of the flower forms the doorstep? How is it marked to show the way in? Which part of the flower makes the arch above the door?

2. Find the anther, and describe how it is placed. Can you see two nectar-wells? Explain how a bee will become dusted with pollen while getting the nectar.

3. Where is the stigma? What is there very peculiar about the styles of the iris? Can a bee, when backing out from the side door, dust the stigma with the pollen she has just swept off? Why not? How does the stigma of the next flower that the bee visits get some of the pollen from her back?

4. Look straight down into an iris flower. Can you see the three petals? How are they marked? How would these lines on the petals mislead any insect that was searching for nectar?

5. Watch the insects visiting the iris. Do you know what they are? What do they do?

6. Describe the way the iris flower-bud is enfolded in bracts. What is there peculiar about the way the iris leaves join the stem?

7. How many kinds of flag, or iris, do you know?

8. Describe the seed-vessel and seeds of the iris.

"It is said that the Franks of old had a custom, at the proclamation of a king, of elevating him upon a shield or target, and placing in his hand a reed, or flag in blossom, instead of a sceptre."

—AMONG THE FLOWERS AND TREES WITH THE POETS, WAIT AND LEONARD.

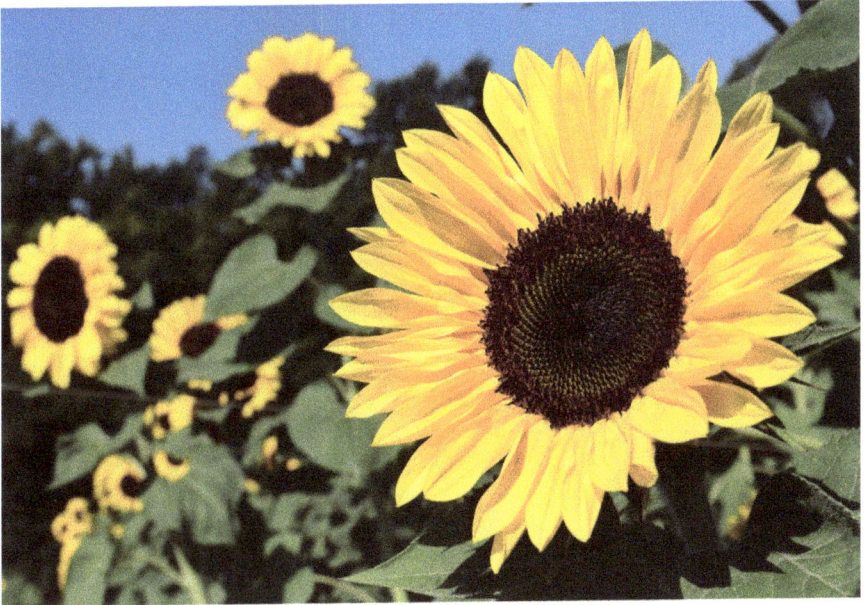

The Sunflower

MANY of the most beautiful of the autumn flowers belong to the *Compositae*, a family of such complicated flower arrangement that it is very difficult for the child or the beginner in botany to comprehend it; and yet, when once understood, the composite scheme is very simple and beautiful, and is repeated over and over in flowers of very different appearance. It is a plan of flower cooperation; there are many flowers associated to form a single flower-head. Some of these, the "ray," or "banner," flowers, hold out bright pennants to attract the attention of insects; while the disk-flowers, which they surround, attend to the matter of the pollenation and production of seed.

The large garden sunflower is the teacher's ally to illustrate to the children the story of the composites. Its florets are so large that it is like a great wax model. And what could be more interesting than to watch its beautiful inflorescence—that orderly march toward the center in double lines of anther columns, with phalanxes bearing the stigmas surrounding them; and outside all, the ranks of ray-flowers

The sunflower. Next to the ray-flowers are the florets in last stages of blossoming with stigmas protruding; next within are rows in the earlier stage with pollen bursting from anther-tubes, while at the center are the unopened buds.

flaunting their flags to herald to the world this peaceful conquest of the sleeping, tented buds at the center?

Ordinarily, in nature-study we do not pull the flowers apart, as is necessary in botany; in nature-study, all that we care to know of the flower is what it does, and we can see that without dissection. But with the compositae the situation is quite different. Here we have an assemblage of flowers, each individual doing its own work for the community; and in order to make the pupils understand this fact it is necessary to study the individual florets.

We begin with the study of one of the buds at the center of the flower-head; this shows the white, immature seed below, and the closed, yellow corolla-tube above. Within the corolla may be seen the brown anther-tube, and on the upper part of the seed are two little, white, earlike scales, to which especial notice should be directed, since in other composites there are many of these scales and they form the pappus—the balloon to carry the seed. The bud shows best the protecting chaffy scale which enfolds the seed, its pointed, spine-edged tip being folded over the young bud, as may be seen by examining carefully the center of a freshly opened sunflower. In this tubular bud, there is a telescopic arrangement of the organs, and one after another is pushed out. First, the corolla-tube opens, starlike, with five pointed lobes, very pretty and graceful, with a bulblike base; from this corolla pushes out the dark-brown tube, made up of five anthers grown together. By opening the corolla, we see the filaments of the stamens below the joined anthers. This anther tube, if examined through a lens, shows rows of tiny points above and below, two to each anther, as if they had been opened like a book to join edges with their neighbors. The anther-tube is closed at the tip, making a five-sided cone; and at the seams, the yellow pollen bulges out, in starlike rays. The pollen bulges out for good reason, for behind it is the stigma, like a ramrod, pushing all before it in the tube for it is its turn next to greet the outer world. The two stigma-lobes are pressed together like the halves of a sharpened pencil, and they protrude through the anther-tube as soon as all the pollen is safely pushed out; then the stigma-lobes separate, each curling backwards so as to offer a receptive surface to welcome pollen grains from other florets, or even other sunflowers. In the process of curling back, they press the anther-tube down into the corolla, and thus make the floret shorter than when in the pollen stage. The banner-flower differs in many essentials from the perfect florets of the disk. If we remove one from the flower-head, we find at its base a seedlike portion, which is a mere pretense; it is shrunken, and never can be a seed because it has connected with it no stigma to bring to it the pollen. Nor does this flower have stamens nor a tubular corolla; instead it has one great, petallike banner, many times longer and wider than the corollas of the other flowers. All this flower has to do is to hold its banner aloft as a sign to the world, especially the insect world, that here is to be found pollen in plenty, and nectar for the probing.

But more wonderful than the perfection of each floret is their arrangement in the flower-head. Around the edge of the disk the banner-flowers, in double or treble rank, flare wide their long petals like the rays of the sun, making the sunflower a most striking object in the landscape. If the sunflower has been open for several days, next to the ray-flowers will be seen a circle of star-mouthed corollas from which both ripened pollen and stigmas have disappeared, and the

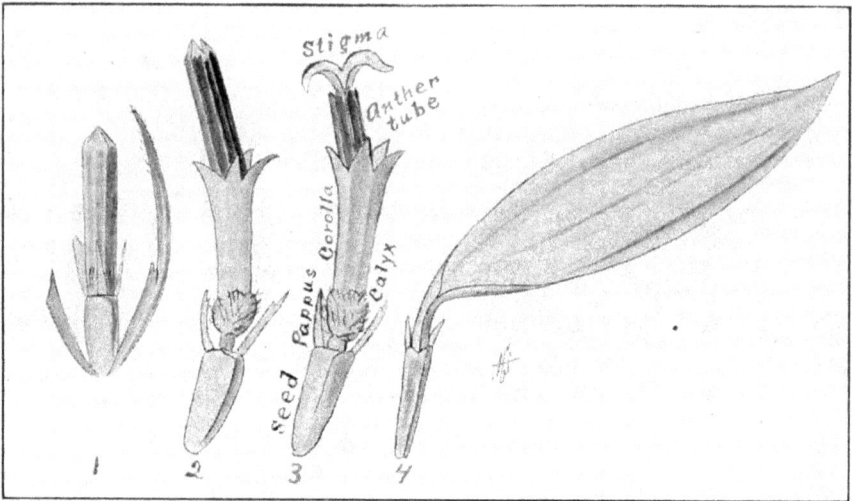

The flower of the sunflower-head enlarged.
1. A floret of the sunflower in the bud-stage as it appears at the center of the sunflower. Note the protecting bract at the right.
2. A floret in earliest stage of blossoming.
3. A floret in the latest stage of bloom with the parts named.
4. A ray or banner-flower.

fertilized seeds below them are attaining their growth. Next comes a two or three-ranked circle, where the split, coiled-back stigma-lobes protrude from the anther-tubes; within this circle may be two or three rows of florets, where pollen is being pushed out in starry radiance; and within this ring there may be a circle where the anther-tubes are still closed; while at the center lie the buds, arranged in exquisite pattern of circling radii, cut by radii circling in the opposite direction; and at the very center the buds are covered with the green spear-points of their bracts. I never look at the buds in the sunflower without wondering if the study of their arrangement is not the basis of much of the most exquisite decoration in Moorish architecture. To appreciate fully this procession of the bloom of the sunflower from its rim to its center, we need to watch it day by day—then only can its beauty become a part of us.

The great, green bracts, with their long pointed tips, which "shingle" the house of every sunflower family, should be noted with care, because these bracts have manifold forms in the great *Compositae* family; and the pupil should learn to recognize this part of the flower-head, merely from its position. In the burdocks, these bracts form the hooks which fasten to the passer-by; in the thistle, they form the prickly vase about the blossom; while in the pearly everlasting, they make the beautiful, white, shell-like mass of the flower which we treasure as immortal. In the sunflower, these bracts are very ornamental, being feltlike outside and very smooth inside, bordered with fringes of pretty hairs, which may be seen best through a lens. They overlap each other regularly in circular rows, and each bract is bent so as to fit around the disk.

In looking at a mass of garden sunflowers, we are convinced that the heavy heads bend the stems, and this is probably true, in a measure. But the stems are very solid and firm, and the bend is as stiff as the elbow of a stovepipe; and after examining it, we are sure that this bend is made with the connivance of the stem, rather than despite it. Probably most people, the world over, believe that sunflowers twist their stems so that their blossoms face the sun all day. This belief shows the utter contentment of most people with a pretty theory. If you believe it, you had best ask the first sunflower you see if it is true, and she will answer you if you will ask the question morning, noon and night. My own observations make me believe that the sunflower, during the later weeks of its bloom, is like the Mohammedan, keeping

A field of sunflowers

its face toward the east. True, I have found many exceptions to this rule, although I have seen whole fields of sunflowers facing eastward, when the setting sun was gilding the backs of their great heads. If they do turn with the sun, it must be in the period of earliest blossoming before they become heavy with ripening seeds.

The sunflower seed is eagerly sought by many birds, and it is raised extensively for chicken-feed. The inadequate little pappus falls off, and the seeds are set, large end up, in the very ornamental diamond-shaped sockets. They finally become loosened, and now we see a reason for the bending flower-head; for, as the great stem is assaulted by the winds of autumn, the bended heads shake out their seed and scatter them far afield.

LESSON

Leading thought— The sunflower is not a single flower, but is a large family of flowers living together; and each little flower, or floret, as it is called, has its own work to do for the family welfare.

Method— Early in September, when school first opens, is the time for this lesson. If sunflowers are growing near by, they should be studied where they stand; and their story may thus be more completely told. Otherwise, a sunflower should be brought to the schoolroom and placed in water. If one is selected which has just begun to blossom, it will show, day by day, the advance of the blossoming ranks. I have kept such a flower fourteen days, and it blossomed cheerfully from its rim to its very center. A large sunflower that has only partially blossomed is also needed for taking apart to show the arrangement of this big flower-family. Take a bud from the center, a floret showing anther-tube and another showing the curled pair of stigmas, and a ray or banner-flower. Each pupil should be furnished with these four florets; and after they have studied them, show them the other half of the sunflower, with each floret in place. After this preliminary study, let them observe the blossoming sunflower for several consecutive days.

Observations—

1. A little flower which is part of a big flower-family is called a floret. You have before you three florets of a sunflower and a banner-flower. Study first the bud. Of how many parts is it composed? What will the lower, white part develop into? Can you see two little white points standing up from it on each side of the bud? Note the shape and color of the unopened floret. Note that there is a narrow, stiff, leaf-like bract, which at its base clasps the young seed, while its pointed tip bends protectingly over the top of the bud.

2. Take an open floret with the long, dark brown tube projecting from it. Note that the young seed is somewhat larger than in the bud, and that it still has its earlike projections at the top. Describe the shape of the open corolla. Look at the brown tube with a lens. How many sides has it? How many little points projecting at the top and bottom on each side of the tube? How does the tube look at the tip, through a lens? Can you see the pollen bursting out? If so, how does it look? Do you think that there is just one tubular anther, or do you think several anthers are joined together to make this tube? Open the corolla-tube carefully, and see if you can answer this last question. Open the anther-tube, and see if you can find the pistil with its stigmas.

3. Take a floret with the two yellow horns of the stigma projecting.

Where is the brown anther-tube now? Is it as long as in the floret you have just studied? What has happened to it? What did the stigmas do to the pollen in the anther-tube? How do the two parts or lobes of the stigma look when they first project? How later?

4. Make a banner-flower. How many parts are there to it? How does the seedlike portion of the blossom look? Do you think it will ever be a good seed? Describe the corolla of this flower. How much larger is it than the corolla of the florets? Has the banner-flower any pistil or stamens? Of what use is the banner-flower to the sunflower family? Do you think that we would plant sunflowers in our gardens for their beauty if they had no banner-flowers?

5. After studying the separate flowers, study a sunflower in blossom, and note the following: Where are the banner-flowers placed? How many rows are there? How are they set so that their banners make the sunflower look like the sun? Do you see why the central portion of the sunflower is called the disk, and the banner-flowers are called the rays—in imitation of the sun?

6. Next to the banner-flowers, what sort of florets appear? How many rows are there? What kind form the next circle, and in how many rows? What stages of the florets do you find forming the inner circle, and how many rows? What do you find at the center of the flower-head? Note the beautiful pattern in which the buds are arranged. Can you see the separate buds at the very center of the sunflower? If not, why?

7. Make notes on a sunflower that has just opened, describing the stages of the florets that are in blossom; continue these notes every day for a week, describing, each day, what has happened. If the sunflower you are observing is in garden or field, note how many days elapse between the opening of the outer row of flowers and the opening of the central buds.

8. Look below or behind the sunflower, and note the way it is attached to the stem. What covers the disk? These green, overlapping, leaflike structures are called bracts. What is the shape of one of these bracts? What is its texture, outside and inside? Look at it, with a lens, along the edges, and note what you see. How are the bracts arranged? Do they not "shingle" the house in which the sunflower-family lives?

This covering of the disk, or the house where the sunflower-family lives, is called the involucre.

9. Does the stem of the sunflower hold it upright? Some people declare that it twists its stem so as to face the sun all day. Do you think this is true?

10. Study a sunflower-head after the seeds are ripe. Do the little ears which you saw at the top of the seeds still remain? How does the sunflower scatter the seeds? Note how the disk looks after the seeds are all gone. What birds are especially fond of sunflower seeds? Of what use are the seeds commercially?

"Flowers have an expression of countenance as much as men or animals. Some seem to smile; some have a sad expression; some are pensive and diffident; others again are plain, honest, and upright, like the broad-faced Sunflower, and the hollyhock."

—HENRY WARD BEECHER.

"Eagle of flowers! I see thee stand,
And on the sun's noon-glory gaze;
With eye like his thy lids expand
And fringe their disk with golden rays;
Though fixed on earth, in darkness rooted there,
Light is thy element, thy dwelling air,
Thy prospect heaven."

—"THE SUNFLOWER," MONTGOMERY.

The Bachelor's Button

TEACHER'S STORY

THIS beautiful garden flower gives a variation in form from other composites when studied according to the Lesson for a Composite Flower on page 91. This valued garden flower came to us from Europe and it sometimes escapes cultivation and runs wild in a gentle way. We call it bachelor's button; but in Europe it is called the cornflower, and under this name it found its way into literature. None of the flowers that live in families repays close study better than does the bachelor's button. The ray-flowers are tubular but they do not have banners. Their tubes flare open like trumpets, and they are indeed color trumpets heralding to the insect world that there is nectar for the probing and pollen for exchange. Looked at from above, the ray-flowers do not seem tubular; from the sides, they show as uneven-mouthed trumpets with lobed edges; but though we search each trumpet to its slender depths we can find no pistils. These ray-flowers have no duty in the way of maturing seeds.

Stigma open and showing pollen-brush below. Enlarged

In some varieties the ray-flowers are white, and in others they are blue and purple. They vary in number from 7 to 14, or more.

The disk-flowers have a long corolla-tube, which is white and delicately lobed and is enlarged toward the upper end to a purple bulb with five, long, slender lobes. The anther-tube is purplish black, and is bent into almost a hook, the tip opening toward the middle of the flower-head. The pollen is glistening white tinged with yellow, and looks very pretty as it bursts out from the dark tubes. The purple stigma first appears with its tips close together, but with a pollen brush just below it; later it opens into a short Y. The buds at the center of the flower are bent hook-shaped over the center of the flower-head. The involucral bracts or "shingles" are very pretty, each one ornamented with a scaly fringe; they form a long, elegantly shaped base to the flower-head. After the flowers have gone and the seeds have ripened, these bracts flare open, making a wide-mouthed urn from which the ripened seeds are shaken by the winds; and after the seeds are gone, the white fuzz of their empty cases remains at the bottom of the urn. The seed is plump and shining, with a short fringe of pappus around the top and a contracted place at one side near the base where it grew fast to the receptacle; for these seeds are not set on end, as are those of the sunflower. The short pappus is hardly sufficient to buoy up the seed, and yet undoubtedly aids it to make a flying jump with the passing breeze.

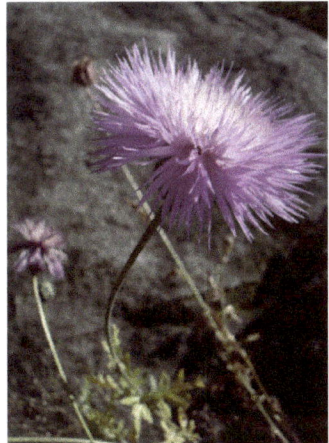

EPIBASE (CC BY 3.0)
Sweet sultan. This flower comes in many shades

LESSON

Leading thought— Each bachelor's button is made up of many little flowers which may be studied by the outline given in Lesson for a Composite Flower on page 91.

67

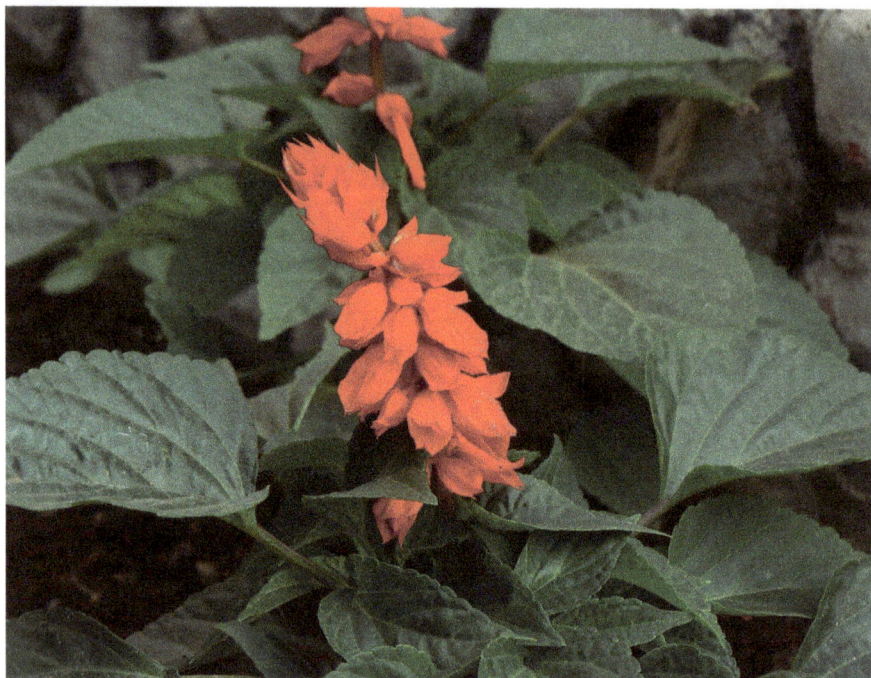

The Salvia, or Scarlet Sage

TEACHER'S STORY

THE flower story of the sage is so peculiar that Darwin has used it to illustrate the mechanisms present in some flowers which the visiting insects must work in order to get the nectar. The scarlet sage, which gladdens our flower beds during the summer and autumn with its brilliance, has as interesting a story as has any of its family. Looking at it from the outside, we should say that its nectar-wells lie too deep to be reached by any insect except a moth or butterfly, or a humming bird; there is no platform for a bee to alight upon, and the tube is too long to be fathomed by a bee's tongue; but the bees are very good business folk; they adapt themselves to flowers that are not adapted to them, and in autumn the glow of the salvia attracts the eye scarcely more than the hum of the visiting bees attracts the ear.

The calyx of the salvia is as red as the corolla, and is somewhat fuzzy while the corolla is smooth. The calyx is a three-lobed bulging tube held stiff by rather strong veins; there is one large lobe above and two small ones below the corolla. The corolla is a tube which is more than twice the length of the calyx; it is prolonged above into a projecting hood, which holds the anthers and the stigma; it has a short, cuplike lower lip and two little turned-back, earlike lobes at the side.

The special mechanism of the salvia is shown in the stamens; there are two of these lying flat along the floor of the corolla-tube and grown fast to it. Near the mouth of the tube, each of these

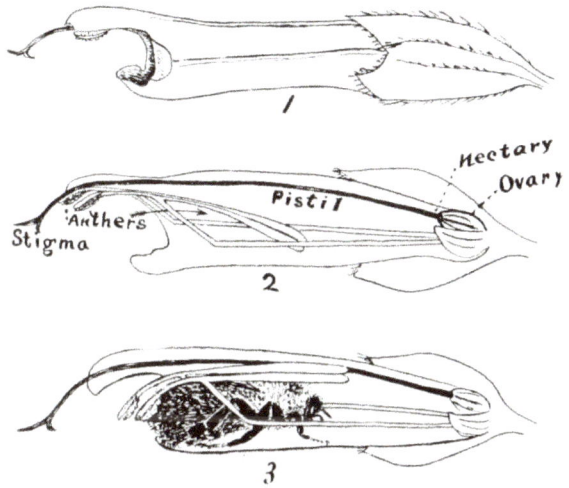

1. Blossom of scarlet sage as seen from outside.
2. The same flower with side removed showing the arrangement of its parts.
3. A bee working the stamen's mechanism as she seeks the nectar.

GIDIP (CC BY-SA 3.0)

lifts up at a broad angle to the roof, and is more or less T-shaped; at the tip of one of the arms of the T is an anther while the other arm is longer and slants down and inward to the floor of the tube, as shown at 2 in the figure.

The bee visiting the flower and entering the corolla-tube, pushes her head against the inner arms of the stamens, lifting them, and in

69

so doing causes the anthers on the front arms of the T to lower and leave streaks of pollen along her fuzzy sides. The stigma is at first concealed in the hood; but, when ripe, it projects and hangs down in front of the opening of the corolla-tube, where it may be brushed along one side or the other by the visiting insect, which has been dusted with the pollen of some other flower. The stigma-lobes open in such a manner that they do not catch the pollen from the insect backing out of their own corolla. As the nectar is at the base of the corolla-tube, the bees, in order to get it, crawl in almost out of sight. Late in the season they seem to "go crazy" when gathering this nectar; I have often seen them searching the bases of the corolla-tubes which have fallen to the ground, in order to get what is left of the sweet treasure.

But the pollen story is not all that is of interest in the salvia. Some of the parts of the flower which are green in most blossoms, are scarlet as a cardinal's robe in this. If we glance at a flower stalk, we see that at its tip it looks like a braided, flattened cone; this appearance is caused by the scarlet, long-pointed bracts, each of which covers, with its bulging base, the scarlet calyx which in turn enfolds the scarlet flower bud. These bracts fall as the flowers are

The salvia, or scarlet sage, showing the bracts still present above and falling as the flowers open

ready to open, making a brilliant carpet about the plant. Each flower stem continues to develop buds at its tip for a long season; and this, taken together with its scarlet bracts and flowers, renders the salvia a thing of beauty in our gardens, and makes it cry aloud to pollen-carriers that here, even in late autumn, there is plenty of nectar.

LESSON

Leading thought— This flower has the bracts and calyx scarlet instead of green, and this makes it a brilliant mass of color to please our eyes and attract the pollen-carrying insects. Its anthers are arranged at the tip of two levers, which the insects push up and down as they enter the flower, thus becoming dusted with pollen.

Method— The structure of this flower may be studied in the schoolroom and its mechanism there understood; but the most important part of the lesson is the observation out-of-doors upon the way the bees work the stamen levers when seeking the nectar. This is best observed during late September or October, after other flowers are mostly gone, and when the bees are working with frantic haste to get all the honey possible.

Observations—

1. How does the calyx of the salvia differ from that of other flowers in color? How does it differ from the corolla in texture? How many lobes has it? How are they placed about the corolla?

2. What is the shape of the corolla? How does it make a hood over the entrance to the tube? What does the hood hold? Is there any platform made by the lower lip of the corolla for a visiting insect to alight upon?

3. Cut open one side of the corolla and describe how the stamens are arranged. Thrust your pencil into an uninjured flower and see if the anthers in the hood are moved by it. How? Describe how a bee in visiting this flower moves the anthers so as to become dusted with pollen.

4. Where is the stigma? How does it receive pollen from visiting insects? Would it be likely to get the pollen which has just been scraped off from its own anthers by the bee? Why?

Salvia in a flower garden

5. Experiment to find where the nectar is. Do you ever see bees getting the nectar from fallen flowers? Do they get it from the "front" or the "back door?"

6. What other parts of this flower are red, which in other flowers are green? How does this make the budding portions of the flower stem look? Why does this make the salvia a more beautiful plant for our gardens?

7. Compare the mechanism of the stamens of the scarlet sage with the mechanism of the stamens of the common garden sage.

Petunias

HESE red-purple and white flowers, which, massed in borders and beds, make gay our gardens and grounds in late summer and early autumn, have an interesting history. Professor L. H. Bailey uses it as an illustration in his thought-inspiring book, "The Survival of the Unlike;" he says that our modern petunias are a strange compound of two original species; the first one was found on the shores of the La Plata in South America and was introduced into Europe in 1823. "It is a plant of upright habit, thick sticky leaves and sticky stems, and very long-tubed white flowers which exhale a strong perfume at nightfall." The second species of petunia came from seeds sent from Argentina to the Glasgow Botanical Gardens in 1831. "This is a more compact plant than the other, with a decumbent base, narrower leaves and small, red-purple flowers which have a very broad or ventricose tube, scarcely twice longer than the slender calyx lobes." This plant was called *Petunia violacea* and it was easily hybridized with the white species; it is now, strangely enough, lost to cultivation, although the white species is found in some old gardens. The hybrids of these two species are the ancestors of our garden petunias, which show the purple-red and white of their progenitors. The petunias are of the Nightshade family and are kin to the potato, tomato, egg-plant, tobacco and Jimson-weed, and, like the latter, the flowers are especially adapted to give nectar to the long-tongued sphinx or hummingbird moths.

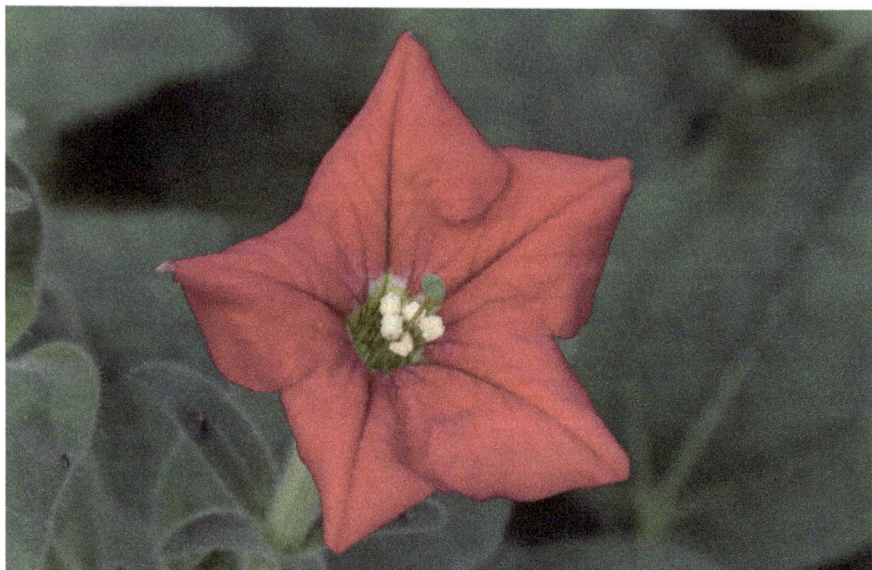

The petunia corolla is tubular, and the five lobes open out in salver-shape; each lobe is slightly notched at its middle, from which point a marked midrib extends to the base of the tube. In some varieties the edges of the lobes are ruffled. Within the throat of the tube may be seen a network of darker veins, and in some varieties this network spreads out over the corolla-lobes. Although many colors have been developed in petunias, the red-purple and white still predominate; when the two colors combine in one flower, the pattern may be symmetrical, but is often broken and blotchy.

When a flower-bud is nearly ready to open the long, bristly tube of the corolla lies with its narrow base set in the calyx, the long, fuzzy lobes of which flare out in bell-shape; the tube is marked by lengthwise lines made by the five midribs; the lobes of the corolla are folded along the outer portions of these midribs, and these folded tips are twisted together much as if some one had given them a half turn with the thumb and finger. It is a pleasing experience to watch one of these flowers unfold. When a flower first opens, there lies near the bottom of the throat of the tube the green stigma, with two anthers snuggled up in front of it and two behind it, the latter being not quite so advanced in age as the former. As the filaments of the front pair of anthers are longer than those of the rear pair, the little group lies at a low angle offering a dusty doormat for entering insects. If we open a flower at this stage, we find another anther, as yet unopened, and which is on the shortest stamen of the five. This seems to be a little pollen-reserve, perhaps for its own use later in the season. There is an interesting mechanism connected with these stamens; each is attached to the corolla-tube at the base for about half its length, and at the

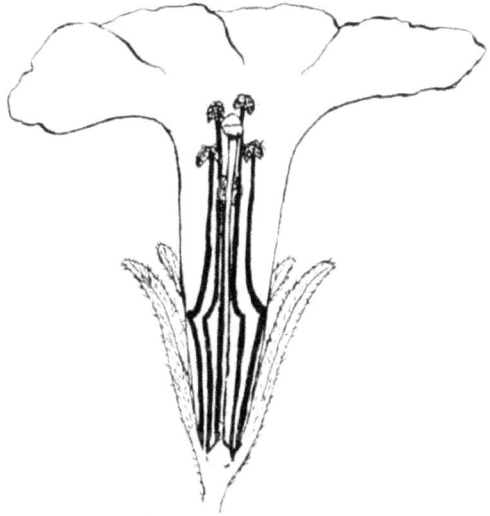

A petunia blossom cut open on the upper side, showing the pistil surrounded by the uncurved stamens and the partially opened stigma surrounded by the anthers. Note the short stamen below the pistil.

point of attachment curves suddenly inward so as to "cuddle up" to the pistil, the base of which is set in the nectar-well at the bottom of the flower. If we introduce a slender pencil or a toothpick into the flower-tube along the path which the moth's tongue must follow to reach the nectar, we can see that the stamens, pressing against it at the point where they curve inward, cause the anthers to move about so as to discharge their pollen upon it; and as the toothpick is withdrawn they close upon it cogently so that it carries off all the pollen with which it is brought in contact.

If we look at the stigma at the center of its anther-guard, it has a certain close-fisted appearance, although its outer edges may be dusted with the pollen; as the flower grows older, the stigma stands above the empty anthers at the throat of the flower tube and opens out into two distinct lobes. Even though it may have accepted some of its own pollen, it apparently opens up a new stigmatic surface for the pollen brought from other flowers by visiting insects.

Dr. James G. Needham says that at Lake Forest he has been attracted to the petunia beds in the twilight by the whirring of the wings of countless numbers of sphinx, or hummingbird moths which were

Starry Night petunia, seen in a Brazilian nursery

visiting these flowers. We also may find these moths hovering over petunia beds in almost any region if we visit them on the warmer evenings. And it is a safe guess that the remote white ancestor of our petunias had some special species of sphinx moth which it depended upon for carrying its pollen; and the strong perfume it exhaled at nightfall was an odor signal to its moth friends to come and feast.

But even though the petunia flowers are especially adapted to the delectation of hummingbird moths, our bees which—like man—have claimed all the earth, will work industriously in the petunias, scrambling into the blossoms with much remonstrating, high-pitched buzzing because of the tight fit, and thus rifle the nectar-wells that were meant for insects of quite different build.

The leaves of the petunia are so broadly ovate as to be almost lozenge-shape, especially the lower ones; they are soft, and have prominent veins on the lower side; they are without stipules, and have short, flat petioles. The stems are soft and fuzzy and are usually decumbent at the base, except the central stems of a stool or clump which, though surrounded by kneeling sisters, seem to prefer to stand up straight.

The flower stems come off at the axils of the leaves, the lower flowers open first. The blossoms remain open about two days; at the first sign of fading, the lobes of the corolla droop dejectedly like a frill that has lost its starch, and finally the corolla—tube and all—drops off, leaving a little conical seed-capsule nestled snugly in the heart of the bell-shaped calyx. At this time, if this peaked cap of the seed-capsule be removed, the many seeds look like tiny white pearls set upon the fleshy, conical placenta. As the capsule ripens, it grows brown and glossy like glazed manila paper and it is nearly as thin; then it cracks precisely down its middle, and the seeds are spilled out at any stirring of the stems. The ripe seeds are dark brown, almost as fine as dust, and yet, when examined with a lens, they are seen to be exquisitely netted and pitted.

References— *The Survival of the Unlike*, L. H. Bailey; *The Encyclopedia of Horticulture*, Bailey; *Our Garden Flowers*, Harriet Keeler.

LESSON

Leading thought— The petunias have an interesting history being native to South America. Their flowers are fitted by form and mechanism to entice the hummingbird moths as visitors, and to use them for carrying pollen.

Method— The petunias are such determined bloomers that they give us flowers up to the time of killing frosts, and they are therefore good material for nature lessons. Each pupil should have a flower in hand to observe during the lesson, and should also have access to a petunia bed for observations on the habits of the plant.

Observations—

1. What colors do you find in the petunia flowers? If striped or otherwise marked, what are the colors? Are the markings symmetrical and regular?

2. Sketch or describe a flower, looking into it. What is the shape of the corolla-lobes? How many lobes are there? How are they veined? What peculiar markings are at the throat of the flower?

3. What are the color and position of the stigma? How are the stamens arranged? How many anthers do you see? What is the color of the anthers? Of the pollen?

4. Sketch or describe the flower from the side. What is the shape of the corolla-tube? Is it smooth or fuzzy? How is it marked? What are the number and shape of the sepals, or lobes, of the calyx?

5. Study a freshly opened flower, and describe the position and

A red and white mixed petunia

appearance of the anthers and stigma. Do they remain in these relative positions after the flower is old?

6. Cut open a flower, slitting it along the upper side. Describe the stamens and how they are attached. Is the pistil attached in the same manner? Where is the nectar? Thrust a slender pencil or a toothpick into the tube of a fresh flower. Does this spread the anthers apart and move them around? When it is withdrawn, is there pollen on it? Can you see in your open flower the mechanism by which the pollen is dusted on the object thrust into the flower?

7. What insects have tongues sufficiently long to reach the nectar-well at the bottom of the petunia flower? At what time do these insects fly? At what time of day do most of the petunia flowers open? Visit the petunia beds in the twilight, and note whether there are any insects visiting them. What insects do you find visiting these flowers during the day?

8. Sketch or describe the leaves of the petunia. How do the leaves feel? Look at a leaf with a lens and note the fringe of hair along its edges. Describe the veining of the leaf.

9. Describe the petunia stems. Are they stout or slender? How do they feel? With what are they covered? Where do the flower stems come off the main stalk?

10. Describe or sketch a flower-bud just ready to open. How are the tips of the lobes folded? How long does the flower remain in bloom? What is the first sign of its fading?

11. Describe the seed-capsule. Where does it open? Are the seeds many or few, large or small? What is their color when ripe? When examined with a lens, have they any pits or markings?

A horseshoe geranium

The Horseshoe Geranium

TEACHER'S STORY

THE geraniums perhaps do more to brighten the world than almost any other cultivated flowers. They will grow for every one, whether for the gardener in the conservatory of the rich, or in a tin can on the windowsill of the crowded tenement of the poor. And it is interesting to know that this common plant has a cultivated ancestry of two hundred years' standing. These geraniums, which are really not geraniums botanically but are *pelargoniums*, originally came from southern Africa, and the two ancestors of our common bedding geraniums were introduced into England in 1710 and 1714.

The geranium is of special value to the teacher, since it is available for study at any season of the year, and has a most interesting blossom. The single-flowered varieties should be used for this lesson, since

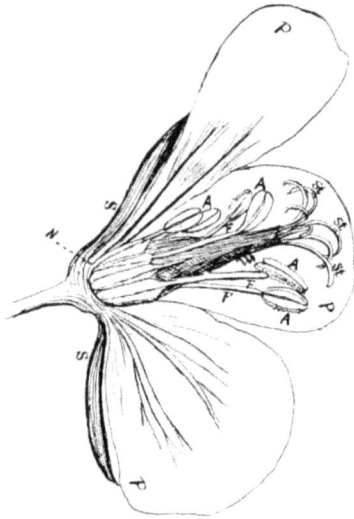

Flower of the horseshoe geranium.
S, sepals; P, petals; A, anther; F, filament; m, pistil; St, stigma; N, opening to nectar tube.

the blossoms that are double have lost their original form. Moreover, the geranium's blossom is so simple that it is of special value as a subject for a beginning lesson in teaching the parts of a flower; and its leaves and stems may likewise be used for the first lessons in plant structure.

The stem is thick and fleshy, and is downy on the new growth; there is much food stored in these stems, which accounts for the readiness with which cuttings from them will grow. Wherever a leaf comes off the stem, it is guarded by two stipules at the base; these stipules often remain after the leaves have fallen, thus giving the stem an unkempt look. The leaves are of various shapes, although of one general pattern; they are circular and beautifully scalloped and lobed, with veins for every lobe radiating from the petiole; they are velvety above and of quite different texture beneath, and many show the dark horseshoe which gives the name to this variety. The petiole is usually long and stiff and the leaves are set alternately upon the stem.

The flower has five petals, and at first glance they seem of much the same shape and position; but if we look at them carefully, we see that the upper two are much narrower at the base and project farther forward than do the lower three. Moreover, there are certain lines on these upper petals all pointing toward the center of the flower; these are the nectar guide-lines, and if we follow them we find a deep nectar-well just at the base of these upper petals and situated above the ovary of the flower. No other flower shows a prettier plan for guiding insects to the hidden sweets, and in none is there a more obvious and easily seen well of nectar. It extends almost the whole length of the flower stem, the nectar gland forming a hump near the base of the stem. If we thrust a needle down the whole length of this nectar tube we can see that this bright flower developed its nectar especially for some long-tongued insect, probably a butterfly. It is interesting to note that in the double geranium where the stamens have been all changed to petals and where, therefore, no seeds are formed, this nectar-well has been lost.

There are five sepals, the lower one being the largest. But the geranium is careless about the number of its sta-

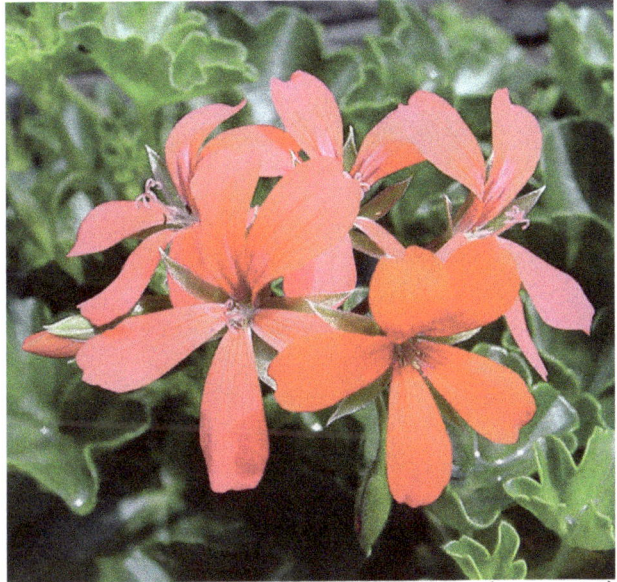

Ivy geranium

mens; most flowers are very good mathematicians, and if they have five sepals and five petals they are likely to have five or ten stamens. The geranium often shows seven anthers, but if we look carefully we may find ten stamens, three of them without anthers. But this is not always true; there are sometimes five anthers and two or three filaments without anthers. The color of the anthers differs with the variety of the flower. The stamens broaden below, and their bases are joined making a cup around the lower part of the ovary. The pistil is at the center of the flower and has no style, but at the summit divides into five long, curving stigmas; but again the geranium cannot be trusted to count, for sometimes there are seven or eight stigmas. Although many of our common varieties of geraniums have been bred so long that they have almost lost the habit of producing seed, yet we may often find in these single blossoms the ovary changed into the peculiar, long, beaklike pod, which shows the relationship of this plant to the cranesbill or wild geranium.

When the buds of the geranium first appear, all of them are nestled in a nest of protecting bracts, each bud being enclosed in its own protecting sepals. But soon each flower stem grows longer and droops

There are many types of geranium

and often the bracts at its base fall off; from this mass of drooping buds, the ones at the center of the cluster lift up and open their blossoms first. Often, when the outside flowers are in bloom, those at the center have withered petals but are hidden by their fresher sisters.

It would be well to say something to the pupils about those plants which have depended upon man so long for their planting that they do not develop any more seed for themselves. In connection with the geraniums, there should be a lesson on how to make cuttings and start their growth. The small side branches or the tips of the main stems may be used as cuttings. With a sharp knife make a cut straight across. Fill shallow boxes with sand, place them in a cool room and keep them constantly moist; plant the cuttings in these boxes, putting the stems for one-third of their length in the sand. After about a month the plants may be repotted in fertile soil. The fall is the best time to make cuttings.

LESSON

Leading thought— The geraniums are very much prized as flowers for ornamental beds. Let us see why they are so valued.

Method— A variety of geranium with single flowers should be chosen for this purpose, and it may be studied in the schoolhouse window or in the garden. As the parts of this flower are of a very general type, it is an excellent one with which to teach the names and purposes of the flower parts. Each child can make a little drawing of the sepals, petals, stamens and pistil, and label them with the proper names.

Observations—

1. What sort of a stem has the geranium? Is it smooth or downy? What makes the geranium stem look so rough and untidy?

2. Study the leaf. Show by description or drawing its shape, its wings, its veins. What are its colors and texture above? Beneath? Is the petiole long or short? What grows at the base of the petiole where it joins the stem? What marking is there on the leaf, which makes us call this a "horseshoe geranium"? Are there other geraniums with leaves of similar shape that have no horseshoe mark?

3. Study the flower. Are the petals all the same size and shape? How many of them are broad? How many narrow? Do the narrow ones project in front of the others? Do these have guide-lines upon them? Where do these lines point? Find the nectar-well. How deep is it? Does it extend almost the entire length of the flower stem? For what insects must it have been developed? Are there nectar-tubes in the stems of the geraniums with double flowers? Why?

4. How many sepals are there? Are they all the same size? Where is the largest?

5. How many stamens can you see? What is the color of the filaments and of the anthers? How are the stamens joined at their bases? Can you find any stamens without anthers?

6. Where is the pistil situated? Can you see the ovary, or seed-box? How many stigmas? Describe their color and shape.

7. In what part of the flower will the seeds be developed? How does the geranium fruit look? Sketch the pod. Do the geraniums develop many seeds? Why not? Do you know the seed-pod of the wild geranium? If so, compare it with the pod of this plant.

8. Take a flower cluster when the flowers are all in the bud, and note the following: When the buds first appear, what protects them? What becomes of these bracts later? How do the sepals protect the bud? Are the bud stems upright and stiff or drooping? How many buds are there in a cluster?

9. Take notes on successive days as follows: What happens to the stem as the bud gets ready to bloom? Is it a central or an outside blossom that opens first? How many new blossoms are there each day? How long is it from the time that the first bud opens until the last bud of the cluster blossoms? What has this to do with making the geranium a valuable ornamental plant?

10. Make some geranium cuttings, and note how they develop into new plants. Place one of the cuttings in a bottle of water and describe how its roots appear and grow.

"God made the flowers to beautify
The earth, and cheer man's careful mood;
And he is happiest who hath power
To gather wisdom from a flower,
And wake his heart in every hour
To pleasant gratitude."

—WORDSWORTH.

CHIPMUNK_1 (CC BY-SA 3.0)

The Sweet Pea

TEACHER'S STORY

"Here are sweet peas on tip for a flight,
With wings of delicate flush o'er delicate white,
And taper fingers catching at all things,
To bind them all about with tiny rings."

—KEATS.

AMONG the most attractive of the seeds which make up the treasure of the children's seed packets, the sweet peas are of the prettiest. They are smooth, little white or brown globules, marked with a scar on the side, showing where they were attached to the pod. One of these peas divides readily into two sections; and after it has been soaked in water for twenty-four hours, the germ of the future plant may, with the aid of a lens, be seen within it. After planting, the sprout pushes through the seed-coat at a point very near the scar, and leaf shoots emerge from the same place; but the two act very differently. The leaf lifts upward toward the light, and the root plunges down into the soil. As the

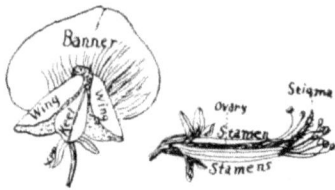

Blossom of sweet pea with parts labelled.

plant grows, it absorbs the food stored in the seed; but the seed remains below ground and does not lift itself into the air, as happens with the bean. The root forms many slender branches, near the tips of which may be seen the fringe of feeding roots, which take up the food and water from the soil. The first leaves of the pea seedling put forth no tendrils, but otherwise look like the later ones. The leaves grow alternately on the stalk, and they are compound, each having from three to seven leaflets. The petiole is winged, as is also the stem of the plant. There is a pair of large, clasping stipules at the base of each leaf. If we compare one of these leaves with a spray of tendrils, we can see that they resemble each other in the following points: The basal leaflets of the petiole are similar and the stipules are present in each case; but the leaflets nearest the tip are marvelously changed to little, stiff stems with a quirl at the tip of each ready to reach out and hook upon any object that offers surface to cling to. Sometimes we find a leaflet paired with a tendril. The sweet pea could not thrive without a support outside of itself.

Of course, the great upper petal of the sweet pea blossom is called the banner! It stands aloft and proclaims the sweet pea as open; but before this occurs, it tenderly enfolds all the inner part of the flower in the unopened bud, and when the flower fades it again performs this duty. The wings are also well named; for these two petals which hang like a peaked roof above the keel, seem like wings just ready to open in flight. The two lower petals are sewed together in one of Nature's invisible seams, making a long, curved treasure chest resembling the keel of a boat, and it has thus been called. Within the keel are hidden the pistil and stamens. The ovary is long, pod-shaped and downy; from its tip the style projects, as strong as a wire, curving upwards, and covered with a brush of fine, white hairs; at the very tip of the style, and often projecting slightly from the keel, is the stigma. Around the sides and below the ovary and style, are nine stamens, their filaments broadening and uniting to make a white, silken tube about the ovary, or young pod. From the tip of this stamen-tube, each of the nine fila-

Sweet pea climbing along a small fence

ments disengages itself, and lying close to the style thrusts its anther up into the point of the keel, below the stigma. But strange to say, one lone, lorn stamen "flocks by itself" above the pistil, curving its anther up stigma-ward. If we touch the point of the keel with the finger, up fly—like a jack-in-the-box—the anthers splashing the finger with pollen; and if a bee, in her search for nectar, alights on the wings at the very base of the petals, up flies the pollen brush and daubs her with the yellow dust, which she may deposit on the stigma of another flower. The interesting part of this mechanism is the brush near the tip of the style below the stigma—a veritable broom, with splints all directed upward. As the pollen is discharged around it, the brush lifts it up when the keel is pressed down, and the stiff petals forming the keel, in springing back to place, scrape off the pollen and plaster it upon the visitor. But for all this elaborate mechanism, sweet peas, of all flowers are the most difficult to cross-pollenate, since they are so likely to receive some of their own pollen during this process.

The sweet-pea bud droops, a tubular calyx with its five-pointed lobes forming a bell to protect it. Within the bud the banner petal clasps all in its protecting embrace.

After the petals fall, the young pod stands out from the calyx, the five lobes of which are recurved and remain until the pod is well grown. As the sweet pea ripens, all the moisture is lost and the pod becomes dry and hard; through the dampness of dews at night and the sun's heat which warps it by day, finally each side of the pod suddenly coils into a spiral, flinging the seed many feet distant in different directions.

Sweet pea pod bursting in spiral

LESSON

Leading thought— The sweet pea has its leaflets changed to tendrils, which hold it to the trellis. Its flower is like that of the clover, the upper petal forming the banner, the two side petals the wings, and the two united lower petals the keel which protects the stamens and pistil.

Method— This should be a garden lesson. A study should be made of the peas before they are planted, and their germination carefully watched. Later, the method of climbing, the flower and the fruit should each be the subject of a lesson.

Observations on germination—

1. Soak some sweet peas over night; split them the next morning. Can you see the little plant within?

2. Plant some of the soaked peas in cotton batting, which may be kept moist. At what point does the sprout break through the seed covering? Do the root and leaf-shoot emerge at the same place, or at different points? Which is the first to appear?

3. Plant some of the soaked peas in the garden. How do the young plants look when they first appear? Does the fleshy part of the seed remain a part of the plant and appear above the ground, as is the case with the bean? What becomes of the meat of the seed after growth has started?

4. Do the first leaves which unfold from the seed pea look like the later ones? Are the leaves simple or compound? Do they grow opposite each other or alternately?

5. Take a leaf and also a spray of the tendrils. How many leaflets

are there in a compound leaf? Describe the petiole and the basal leaves. How far apart are the leaflets on the mid-stem? Compare the stem on which the tendrils grow with this leaf. Are the basal leaflets like those of the leaf? Is the petiole like that of the leaf? Do you think that the leaflets toward the tip of the stem often change to tendrils? Why do you think so? Why must the sweet pea have tendrils? Do you see the earlike stipules at the base of the leaf? Are there similar stipules at the base of the tendril stem?

White sweet pea

Observations on the flower and fruit—

1. Take the sweet pea in blossom. Why is the large upper petal called the banner? How does it compare in size with the other petals? What is its purpose when the flower is open? Why do you think the side petals are called wings? What is their position when the flower is open?

2. Describe that part of the flower below the wings. Do you think that it is made of two petals grown together? Why is it called the keel of the flower? Press down with your finger on the tip of the keel. What happens? Is your finger splashed with pollen? Where is the nectar in the sweet pea? Would an insect getting the nectar press down upon the keel and receive a splash of pollen?

3. Open the keel. How many stamens do you find within it? How many have their filaments joined together? Is there one separate from the others? Against what are the anthers pressed by the keel?

4. Remove the stamens and describe the pistil. Which part of this will make the pod in which the new peas will develop? Describe how the style is curved. How is the style covered near its tip? What is this

brush for? Can you find the stigma with the help of the lens? When the bee is seeking for nectar and pushes down on the keel, does the stigma push out at the same point as the pollen? Does this enable the stigma sometimes to receive pollen which the bees bring from other flowers?

5. Describe an unopened flower bud. What is its position? How many lobes to the calyx? What is their shape, and how do they protect the bud? Which petal is folded over all the others? How does the position of the open flower differ from that of the bud?

A beautiful sweet pea

6. How does the young pod look when the petals fall? How does it look when ripe? How does it open to scatter little, ripe sweet peas? Do the lobes of the sepals still remain with the pod?

Daisies and grasses in a field

A Type Lesson for a Composite Flower

Leading thought— Many plants have their flowers set close together to make a mass of color, like the geraniums or the clovers. But there are other plants where the flowers of one flower-head act like the members of a family, those at the center doing a certain kind of work for the production of seed, and those around the edges doing another kind of work. The sunflower, goldenrod, asters, daisies, cone-flower, thistle, dandelion, burdock, everlasting, and many other common flowers have their blossoms arranged in this way. Before any of the wild-flower members of this family are studied, the lesson on the garden sunflower should be given. (See Sunflowers Lesson on page 62).

Method— These flowers may be studied in the schoolroom with suggestions for field observations. A lens is almost necessary for the study of most of these flowers.

Observations—

1. Can you see that what you call the flower consists of many flowers set together like a beautiful mosaic? Those at the center are called disk-flowers; those around the edges banner or ray-flowers.

2. Note that the flowers around the edges have differently shaped corollas than those at the center. How do they differ? Why should these be called the banner flowers? Why should they be called the ray-flowers? How many banner-flowers are there in the flower family you are studying? How are the banners arranged to make the flower-head more attractive? Cut off or pull out all the banner-flowers and see how the flower-head looks. What do the banner-flowers hold out their

banners for? Is it to attract us or the insects? Has the banner-flower any stigma or stamens?

3. Study the flowers at the center. Are they open, or are they unfolded, buds? Can you make a sketch of how they are arranged? Are any of the florets open? What is the shape and the color of the corolla? Can you see the stamen-tubes pushing out from some? What color are the stamen-tubes? Can you see the two-parted stigmas in others? What color is the pollen? Do the florets at the center or at the outside of the disk open first? When they first open, do you see the stamen-tube or the stigma?

4. The flower-heads are protected before they open with overlapping bracts, which may be compared to a shingled house protecting the flower family. As the flower-head opens, these bracts are pushed back beneath it. Describe the shape of these bracts. Are they set in regular, overlapping rows? Are they rough or smooth? Do they end bluntly, with a short point, with a long point, with a spine, or a hook? How do the bracts act when the flower family goes to sleep? Do they remain after the seeds are ripened?

5. Take a flower-head apart, and examine the florets. Can you see what part of the floret will be the seed? Is there a fringe of pappus above it? If so, what will this be on the seed?

6. Study the ripe seeds. How are they scattered? Do they have balloons? Is the balloon close to the seed? Is it fastened to all parts of it?

TREES

A tree showing the effect of prevailing winds from one direction

Tree Study

TEACHER'S STORY

"I wonder if they like it—being trees?
I suppose they do.
It must feel so good to have the ground so flat,
And feel yourself stand straight up like that.
So stiff in the middle, and then branch at ease,
Big boughs that arch, small ones that bend and blow,
And all those fringy leaves that flutter so.
You'd think they'd break off at the lower end
When the wind fills them, and their great heads bend.
But when you think of all the roots they drop,
As much at bottom as there is on top,
A double tree, widespread in earth and air,
Like a reflection in the water there."
—"TREE FEELINGS" BY CHARLOTTE PERKINS STETSON.

An avenue of trees

NATURAL is our love for trees! A tree is a living being, with a life comparable to our own. In one way it differs from us greatly: it is stationary, and it has roots and trunk instead of legs and body; it is obliged to wait to have what it needs come to it, instead of being able to search the wide world over to satisfy its wants.

THE PARTS OF THE TREE

The *head*, or *crown*, is composed of the branches as a whole, which in turn are composed of the larger and smaller branches and twigs. The *spray* is the term given to the outer twigs, the finest divisions of the trunk, which bear the leaves and fruit. The branches are divisions of the *bole*, or *trunk*, which is the body, or stem, of the tree. The bole, at the base, divides into roots, and the roots into rootlets, which are covered with roothairs. It is important to understand what each of the parts of a tree's anatomy does to help carry on the life of the tree.

The roots, which extend out in every direction beneath the surface

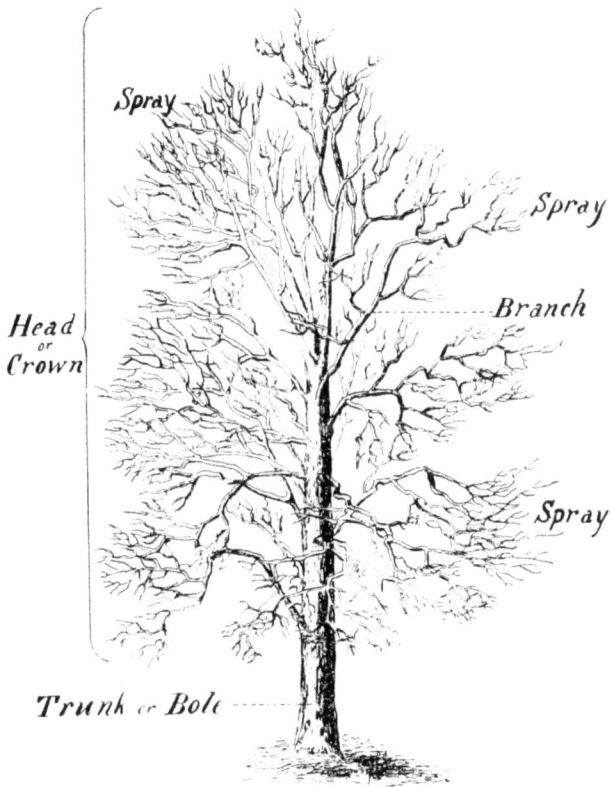

A tree with parts named.

of the ground, have two quite different offices to perform: First, they absorb the water which contains the tree food dissolved from the soil; second, they hold the tree in place against the onslaught of the winds. If we could see a tree standing on its head with its roots spread in the air in the same manner as they are in the ground, we could then better understand that there is as much of the tree hidden below ground as there is in sight above ground, although of quite different shape, being flatter and in a more dense mass. The roots seem to know in which direction to grow to reach water; thus, the larger number of the roots of a tree are often found to extend out toward a stream flowing perhaps some distance from the tree; when they find plenty of food and water the rootlets interlace forming a solid mat. On the Cornell Campus are certain elms which, every six or seven years, completely fill and clog the nearby sewers; these trees send most of their roots in

Annual rings near the center are narrow, but they become much wider.

the direction of the sewer pipe. The fine rootlets upon the tree-roots are covered with root-hairs, which really form the mouths by which the liquid food is taken into the tree.

To understand how firm a base the roots form to hold up the tall trunk, we need to see an uprooted tree. The great roots seem to be molded to take firm grasp upon the soil. It is interesting to study some of the "stump fences" which were made by our forefathers, who uprooted the white pines when the land was cleared of the primeval forest, and made fences of their widespreading but rather shallow extending roots. Many of these fences stand to-day with branching, out-reaching roots, white and weather-worn, but still staunch and massive as if in memory of their strong grasp upon the soil of the wilderness.

The trunk, or bole, or stem of the tree has also two chief offices: It holds the branches aloft, rising to a sufficient height in the forest so that its head shall push through the leaf canopy and expose the leaves to the sunlight. It also is a channel by which the water containing the food surges from root to leaf and back again through each growing part. The branches are divisions of the trunk, and have the same work to do.

Tree roots fighting to hold the riverbank together

In cross-section, the tree trunk shows on the outside the layer of protective bark; next to this comes the cambium layer, which is the vital part of the trunk; it builds on its outside a layer of bark, and on its inside a layer of wood around the trunk. Just within the cambium layer is a lighter colored portion of the trunk, which is called the sap-wood because it is filled with sap which moves up and down its cells in a mysterious manner; the sap-wood consists of the more recent annual rings of growth. Within the sap-wood are concentric rings to the very center or pith; this portion is usually darker in color and is called the heartwood; it no longer has anything to do with the life of the tree, but simply gives to it strength and staunchness. The larger branches, if cut across, show the same structure as the trunk,—the bark on the outside, the cambium layer next, and within this the rings of annual growth. Even the smaller branches and twigs show similar structure, but they are young and have not attained many annual rings.

The leaves are borne on the outermost parts of the tree. A leaf cannot grow, and if it could would be of no use, unless it can be reached by the sunlight. Therefore the trunk lifts the branches aloft, and the branches hold the twigs far out, and the twigs divide into the fine spray, so as to spread the leaves and hold them out into the sunshine.

In structure, the leaf is made up of the stem, or petiole, and the blade, or widened portion of the leaf, which is sustained usually with a framework of many ribs or veins. The petioles and the veins are sap channels like the branches and twigs.

WOOD-GRAIN

This is the way that the sap-river ran
From the root to the top of the tree
Silent and dark,
Under the bark,
Working a wonderful plan
That the leaves never know,
And the branches that grow
On the brink of the tide never see.

—JOHN B. TABB.

THE WAY A TREE GROWS

THE places of growth on a tree may be found at the tips of the twigs and the tips of the rootlets; each year through this growth the tree pushes up higher, down deeper and out farther at the sides. But in addition to all of these growing tips, there is a layer of growth over the entire tree—over every root, over the trunk, over the limbs and over each least twig, just as if a thick coat of paint had been put over the complete tree. It is a coat of growth instead, and these coats of growth make the concentric rings which we see when the trunks or branches are cut across. Such growth as this cannot be made without food; but the tree can take only liquid food from the soil; the root-hairs take up the water in which the "fertilizer" is dissolved, and it is carried up through the larger roots, up through the sap-wood of the trunk, out through the branches to the leaves, where in the leaf-factories the water and free oxygen is given off to the air, and the nourishing elements retained and mixed with certain chemical elements of the air, thus becoming tree food. The leaf is a factory; the green pulp in the leaf cells is part of the machinery; the machinery

Sunlight streaming through pine trees

is set in motion by sunshine power; the raw materials are taken from the air and from the sap containing food from the soil; the finished product is largely starch. Thus, it is well, when we begin the study of the tree, to notice that the leaves are so arranged as to gain all the sunlight possible, for without sunlight the starch factories would be obliged to "shut down." It has been estimated that on a mature maple of vigorous growth there is exposed to the sun nearly a half acre of leaf surface. Our tree appears to us in a new phase when we think of it as a starch factory covering half an acre.

Starch is plant food in a convenient form for storage, and it is stored in sap-wood of the limbs, the branches and trunk, to be used for the growth of the next year's leaves. But starch cannot be assimilated by plants in this form, it must be changed to sugar before it may be used to build up the plant tissues. So the leaves are obliged to perform the office of stomach and digest the food they have made for the tree's use. In the mysterious laboratory of the leaf-cells, the starch is changed to sugar; and nitrogen, sulphur, phosphorus and other substances are taken from the sap and starch added to them, and thus are

Trees in winter

made the proteids which form another part of the tree's diet. It is interesting to note that while the starch factories can operate only in the sunlight, the leaves can digest the food and it can be transported and used in the growing tissues in the *dark*. The leaves are also an aid to the tree in breathing, but they are not especially the lungs of the tree. The tree breathes in certain respects as we do; it takes in oxygen and gives off carbon dioxide; but the air containing the oxygen is taken in through the numerous pores in the leaves called stomata, and also through lenticels in the bark; so the tree really breathes all over its active surface.

The tree is a rapid worker and achieves most of its growth and does most of its work by midsummer. The autumn leaf which is so beautiful has completed its work. The green starch-machinery or chlorophyl, the living protoplasm in the leaf cells, has been withdrawn and is safely secluded in the woody part of the tree. The autumn leaf which glows gold or red, has in it only the material which the tree can no longer use. It is a mistake to believe that the frost causes the brilliant colors of autumn foliage; they are caused by the natural old age and death of the leaves—and where is there to be found old age and death more beautiful? When the leaf assumes its bright colors, it is making ready to depart from the tree; a thin, corky layer is being developed between its petiole and the twig, and when this is perfected, the leaf drops from its own weight or the touch of the slightest breeze.

A tree, growing in open ground, records in its shape, the direction of the prevailing winds. It grows more luxuriantly on the leeward side. It touches the heart of the one who loves trees to note their sturdy endurance of the onslaughts of this, their most ancient enemy.

Reference Books for Tree Study— The Tree Book, Julia Rogers; *Our Native Trees*, Harriet Keeler; *Our Northern Shrubs*, Harriet Keeler; *The Trees of the Northern States*, Romayne Hough. *The Trees*, N. L. Britton; *Getting Acquainted with the Trees*, J. Horace McFarland; *Familiar Trees and their Leaves*, Schuyler Mathews; *Our Trees and How to Know Them*, Clarence Moores Weed; *A Guide to the Trees*, Alice Lounsberry; *The First Book of Forestry*, Filibert Roth; *Practical Forestry*, John Gifford; *Trees in Prose and Poetry*, Stone & Fickett; *The Primers of Forestry*, Pinchot.

As the elevation increases the trees become stunted near the timberline

Acorns

How To Begin Tree Study

TEACHER'S STORY

URING autumn the attention of the children should be attracted to the leaves by their gorgeous colors. It is well to use this interest to cultivate their knowledge of the forms of leaves of trees; but the teaching of the tree species to the young child should be done quite incidentally and guardedly. If the teacher says to the child bringing a leaf, "This is a white oak leaf," the child will soon quite unconsciously learn that leaf by name. Thus, tree study may be begun in the kindergarten or the primary grades.

1. Let the pupils use their leaves as a color lesson by classifying them according to color, and thus train the eye to discriminate tints and color values.

2. Let them classify the leaves according to form, selecting those which resemble each other.

3. Let each child select a leaf of his own choosing and draw it. This may be done by placing the leaf flat on paper and outlining it with pencil or with colored crayon.

4. Let the pupils select paper of a color similar to the chosen leaf and cut a paper leaf like it.

5. Let each pupil select four leaves which are similar and arrange them on a card in a symmetrical design. This may be done while the leaves are fresh, and the card with leaves may be pressed and thus preserved.

Oak leaves

In the fourth grade, begin with the study of a tree which grows near the schoolhouse. In selecting this tree and in speaking of it, impress upon the children that it is a living being, with a life and with needs of its own. I believe so much in making this tree seem an individual, that I would if necessary name it Pocahontas or Martha Washington. First, try to ascertain the age of the tree. Tell an interesting story of who planted it and who were children and attended school in the schoolhouse when the tree was planted. To begin the pupils' work, let each have a little note-book in which shall be written, sketched or described all that happens to this particular tree for a year. The following words with their meaning should be given in the reading and spelling lessons: *Head, bole, trunk, branches, twigs, spray, roots, bark, leaf, petiole, foliage, sap.*

LESSON

Fall (Autumn) Work—

1. What is the color of the tree in its autumn foliage? Sketch it in water colors or crayons, showing the shape of the head, the relative proportions of head and trunk.

2. Describe what you can see of the tree's roots. How far do you suppose the roots reach down? How far out at the sides? In how many ways are the roots useful to the tree? Do you suppose, if the tree were turned bottomside up, that it would show as many roots as it now shows branches?

Fall colors

3. How high on the trunk from the ground do the lower branches come off? How large around is the trunk three feet from the ground? If you know how large around it is, how can you get the distance through? What is the color of the bark? Is the bark smooth or rough? Are the ridges fine or coarse? Are the furrows between the ridges deep or shallow? Of what use is the bark to the tree?

4. Describe the leaf from your tree, paying special attention to its shape, its edges, its color above and below, its veins or ribs, and the relative length and thickness of its petiole. Are the leaves set opposite or alternate upon the twigs? As the leaves begin to fall, can you find two which are exactly the same in size and shape? Draw in your note-book the two leaves which differ most from each other of any that grew on your tree. At what date do the leaves begin to fall from your tree? At what date are they all off the tree?

5. Do you find any fruit or seed upon your tree? If so describe and sketch it, and tell how you think it is scattered and planted.

Winter Study of the Tree—

1. Make a sketch of the tree in your notebook, showing its shape as it stands bare. Does the trunk divide into branches, or does it extend through the center of the tree and the branches come off from its

Trees in winter

sides? Of what use are the branches to a tree? Is the spray, or the twigs at the end of the branches, coarse or fine? Does it lift up or droop? Is the bark on the branches like that on the trunk? Is the color of the spray the same as of the large branches? Why does the tree drop its leaves in winter? Does the tree grow during the winter? Do you think that it sleeps during the winter?

2. Study the cut end of a log or stump and also study a slab. Which is the heart-wood and which is the sap-wood? Can you see the rings of growth? Can you count these rings and tell how old was the tree from which this log came? Describe if you can, how a tree trunk grows larger each year. What is it makes the grain in the wood which we use for furniture? If we girdle a tree why does it die? If we place a nail in a tree three feet from the ground this winter, will it be any higher from the ground ten years from now? How does the tree grow tall?

3. Take a twig of a tree in February and look carefully at the buds. What is their color? Are they shiny, rough, sticky or downy? Are they arranged on the twigs opposite or alternate? Can you see the scar below the buds where the last year's leaf was borne? Place the twig in water and put in a light, warm place, and see what happens to the buds. As the leaves push out, what happens to the scales which protected the buds?

Spring

4. What birds do you find visiting your tree during winter? Tie some strips of beef fat upon its branches, and note all of the kinds of birds which come to feast upon it.

Spring Work—

1. At what date do the young leaves appear upon your tree? What color are they? Look carefully to see how each leaf was folded in the bud. Were all the leaves folded in the same way? Are the young leaves thin, downy and tender? Do they stand out straight as did the old leaves last autumn, or do they droop? Why? Will they change position and stand out as they grow stronger? Why do the leaves stand out from the twigs in order to get sunshine? What would happen to a tree if it lost all its leaves in spring and summer? Tell all of the things you know which the leaves do for the tree.

2. Are there any blossoms on your tree in the spring? If so, how do they look? Are the blossoms which bear the fruit on different trees from those that bear the pollen, or are these flowers placed separately on the same tree? Or does the same flower which produces the pollen also produce the seed? Do the insects carry the pollen from flower to flower, or does the wind do this for your tree? What sort of seeds are formed by these flowers? How are the seeds scattered and planted?

Young leaves and blossoms emerge from buds in spring

3. At what date does your tree stand in full leaf? What color is it now? What birds do you find visiting it? What insects? What animals seek its shade? Do the squirrels live in it?

4. Measure the height of your tree as follows: Choose a bright, sunny morning for this. Take a stick 3 ½ feet long and thrust it in the ground so that three feet will project above the soil. Immediately measure the length of its shadow and of the shadow which your tree makes from its base to the shadow of its topmost twigs. Supposing that the shadow from the stick is 4 feet long and the shadow from your tree is 80 feet long, then your example will be: 4 ft. : 3 ft. :: 80 ft. : ? which will make the tree 60 feet high.

To measure the circumference of the tree, take the trunk three feet from the ground and measure it exactly with a tape measure. To find the thickness of the trunk, divide the circumference just found by 3.14.

Supplementary Reading— Among Green Trees, Rogers; Chap. I in A Primer of Forestry, Pinchot; Part I in A First Book of Forestry, Roth; Chapter IV in Practical Forestry, Gifford.

How To Make Leaf Prints

LESSON

A very practical help in interesting children in trees, is to encourage them to make portfolios of leaf-prints of all the trees of the region. Although the process is mechanical, yet the fact that every print must be correctly labeled makes for useful knowledge. One of my treasured possessions is such a portfolio made by the lads of St. Andrews School of Richmond, Va., who were guided and inspired in this work by their teacher, Professor W. W. Gillette. The impressions were made in green ink and the results are as beautiful as works of art. Professor Gillette gave me my first lesson in making leaf prints.

Material—

1. A smooth slate, or better, a thick plate of glass, about 12 x 15 inches.

2. A tube of printer's ink, either green or black, and costing 50 cents; one tube contains a sufficient supply of ink for making several hundred prints. Or a small quantity of printer's ink may be purchased at any printing office.

3. Two six-inch rubber rollers, such as photographers use in mounting prints, which cost 15 cents each. A letter-press may be used instead of one roller.

4. A small bottle of kerosene to dilute the ink, and a bottle of benzine for cleaning the outfit after using, care being taken to store them safe from fire.

5. Sheets of paper 8 ½ x 11 inches. The paper should be of good quality, with smooth surface in order that it may take and hold a clear outline. The ordinary paper used in printers' offices for printing newspapers works fairly well. I have used with success the paper from blank notebooks which cost five cents a piece.

To make a print, place a few drops of ink upon the glass or slate, and spread it about with the roller until there is a thin coat of ink upon the roller and a smooth patch in the center of the glass or slate. It should never be so liquid as to "run," for then the outlines will be blurred.

NIKA AKIN

Ink the leaf by placing it on the inky surface of the glass and passing the inked roller over it once or twice until the veins show that they are smoothly filled. Now place the inked leaf between two sheets of paper and roll *once* with the *clean* roller, bearing on with all the strength possible; a second passage of the roller blurs the print.

Leaf print of a sycamore maple

Two prints are made at each rolling, one of the upper, and one of the under side of the leaf. Dry and wrinkled leaves may be made pliant by soaking in water, drying between blotters before they are inked.

Prints may also be made a number at a time by pressing them under weights, being careful to put the sheets of paper with the leaves between the pages of old magazines or folded newspapers, in order that the impression of one set of leaves may not mar the others. If a letter-press is available for this purpose, it does the work quickly and well.

SAP
Strong as the sea and silent as the grave,
It flows and ebbs unseen,
Flooding the earth, a fragrant tidal wave,
With mists of deepening green.

—John B. Tabb.

Maple trees tapped to harvest the sap

The Maples

TEACHER'S STORY

HE sugar maple, combining beauty with many kinds of utility, is dear to the American heart. Its habits of growth are very accommodating; when planted where it has plenty of room, it shows a short trunk and oval head, which, like a dark green period, prettily punctuates the summer landscape; but when it occurs in the forest, its noble bole, a pillar of granite gray, rises to uphold the arches of the forest canopy; and it attains there the height of 100 feet. It grows rapidly and is a favorite shade tree, twenty years being long enough to make it thus useful. The foliage is deep green in the summer, the leaf being a glossy, dark green above and paler beneath. It has five main lobes, the two nearest the stem being smaller; the curved edges between the lobes are marked with a few, smoothly cut, large teeth; the main veins extend directly from the petiole to the

The seasonal colors of the sugar maple

sharp tips of the lobes; the petiole is long, slender, and occasionally red. The leaves are placed opposite. The shade made by the foliage of the maple is so dense that it shades down the plants beneath it, even grass growing but sparsely there. If a shade tree stands in an exposed position, it grows luxuriously to the leeward of the prevailing winds, and thus makes a one-sided record of their general direction.

It is its autumn transfiguration which has made people observant of the maple's beauty; yellow, orange, crimson and scarlet foliage make these trees gorgeous when October comes. Nor do the trees get their color uniformly; even in September, the maple will show a scarlet branch in the midst of its green foliage. I believe this is a hectic flush and a premonition of death to the branch which, less vigorous than its neighbors, is being pruned out by Nature's slow but sure method. After the vivid color is on the maple, it begins to shed its leaves. This is by no means the sad act which the poets would have us believe; the brilliant colors are an evidence that the trees have withdrawn from the leaves the green life-substance, the protoplasm-machinery for making the starch, and have stored it snugly in trunk and branch for winter keeping. Thus, only the mineral substances are left in the leaf, and they give the vivid hues. It is a mistake to think that frost causes this brilliance; it is caused by the natural, beautiful, old age of the leaf.

When the leaves finally fall, they form a mulch-carpet for the tree that bore them, and add their substance to the humus from which the tree draws new powers for growth.

After every leaf has fallen, the maple shows why its shade is dense. It has many branches set close and at sharp angles to the trunk, dividing into fine, erect spray, giving the tree a resemblance to a giant whisk-broom. Its dark, deep-furrowed bark smoothes out and becomes light gray on the larger limbs, while the spray is purplish, a color given it by the winter buds. These buds are sharp-pointed and long. In February, their covering of scales shows premonitions of spring by enlarging, and as if due to the soft influence, they become downy, and take on a sunshine color before they are pushed off by the leaves. The leaves and the blossoms appear together. The leaves are at first, yellowish, downy and drooping, thus shunning the too hot sun and the violent pelting rains and fierce spring winds. The flowers appear in tassellike clusters, each downy drooping thread of the tassel bearing at its tip a five-lobed calyx, which may hold seven or eight long, drooping stamens or a pistil with long, double stigmas. The flowers are greenish yellow, and those that bear pollen and those that bear the seeds may be borne on separate trees or on the same tree, but they are always in different clusters. If on the same tree, the seed-bearing tassels are at the tips of the twigs, and those bearing pollen are along the sides.

The ovary is two-celled, but there is usually only one seed developed in the pair which forms a "key"; to observe this, however, we have to dissect the seeds; they have the appearance of two seeds joined together, each provided with a thin, closely veined wing and the two attached to the tree by a single long, drooping stem. This twin-winged form is well fitted to be whirled off by the autumn winds, for the seeds ripen in September. I have seen seedlings growing thickly for rods to the leeward of their parent tree, which stood in an open field. The maples bear blossoms and seeds every year. There are six species of native maples which are readily distinguishable. The silver and the red maples and the box elder are rather large trees; the mountain and the striped (or goosefoot) maples are scarcely more than shrubs, and mostly grow in woods along streams. The Norway and the sycamore maples have been introduced from Europe for ornamental planting. The cut-leaf

Harvesting sap to make maple syrup

silver maple comes from Japan.

The maple wood is hard, heavy, strong, tough and fine-grained; it is cream-color, the heart-wood showing shades of brown; it takes a fine polish and is used as a finishing timber for houses and furniture. It is used in construction of ships, cars, piano action and tool handles; its fine-grained quality makes it good for wood-carving; it is an excellent fuel and has many other uses.

MAPLE-SUGAR MAKING

Although we have tapped the trees in America for many hundred years, we do not as yet understand perfectly the mysteries of the sap flow. In 1903, the scientists at the Vermont Experiment Station did some very remarkable work in clearing up the mysteries of sap movement. Their results were published in their Bulletins 103 and 105, which are very interesting and instructive.

The starch which is changed to sugar in the sap of early spring was made the previous season and stored within the tree. If the foliage of the tree is injured by caterpillars one year, very little sugar can be made from that tree the next spring, because it has been unable to store enough starch in its sapwood and in the outer ray-cells of its smaller branches to make a good supply of sugar. During the latter part of winter, the stored starch disappears, being converted into tree-food in the sap, and then begins that wonderful surging up and down of the sap tide. During the first part of a typical sugar season, more sap comes from above down than from below up; toward the end of the season, during poor sap days, there is more sap coming up from below than down from above. The ideal sugar weather consists of warm days and freezing nights. This change of temperature between day and night acts as a pump. During the day when the branches of the tree are warmed, the pressure forces into the hole bored into the trunk all the sap located in the adjacent cells of the wood. Then the suction which follows a freezing night drives more sap into those cells, which is in turn forced out when the top of the tree is again warmed. The tree is usually tapped on the south side, because the action of the sun and the consequent temperature-pump more readily affects that side.

"Tapping the sugar bush" are magical words to the country boy and girl. Well do we older folk remember those days in March when the south wind settled the snow into hard, marblelike drifts, and the father would say, "We will get the sap-buckets down from the stable loft and wash them, for we shall tap the sugar-bush soon." In those days the buckets were made of staves and were by no means so easily washed as are the

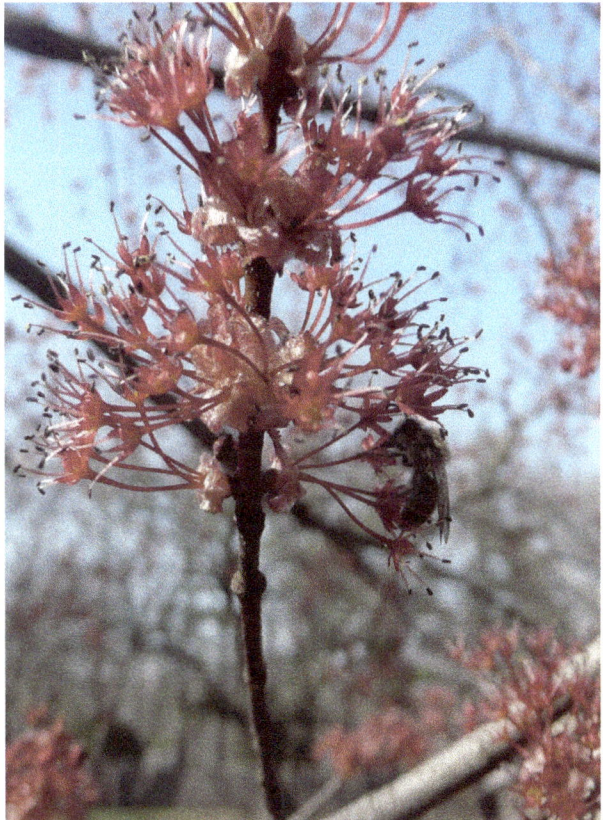

Sugar maple blossoms being visited by a bee

metal buckets of to-day. Well do we recall the sickish smell of musty sap that greeted our nostrils, when we poured in the boiling water to clean those old brown buckets. Previously during the winter evenings, we all had helped fashion sap-spiles from stems of sumac. With buckets and spiles ready when the momentous day came, the large, iron caldron kettle was loaded on a stoneboat together with a sap-cask, log-chain, ax and various other utensils, and as many children as could find standing room; then the oxen were hitched on and the procession started across the rough pasture to the woods, where it eventually arrived after numerous stops for reloading almost everything but the kettle.

When we came to the boiling place, we lifted the kettle into position and flanked it with two great logs against which the fire was to be kindled. Meanwhile the oxen and stoneboat returned to the house for a load of buckets. The oxen blinking, with bowed heads, or with noses lifted aloft to keep the underbrush from striking their faces, "gee'd and haw'd" up hill and down dale through the woods, stopping here and there while the men with augers bored holes in certain trees near other holes which had bled sweet juices in years gone by. When the auger was withdrawn, the sap followed it, and enthusiastic young tongues met it half way, though they received more chips than sweetness therefrom; then the spiles were driven in with a wooden mallet.

The next day after "tapping," those of us large enough to wear the neck-yoke donned cheerfully this badge of servitude and with its help brought pails of sap to the kettle, and the "boiling" began. As the evening shades gathered, how delicious was the odor of the sap steam, permeating the woods farther than the shafts of firelight pierced the gloom! How weird and delightful was this night experience in the woods! And how cheerfully we swallowed the smoke which the contrary wind seemed ever to turn toward us! We poked the fire to send the sparks upward, and now and then added more sap from a barrel, and removed the scum from the boiling liquid with a skimmer thrust into the cleft of a long stick for a handle. As the evening wore on, we drew closer to each other as we told stories of the Indians, bears, panthers and wolves which had roamed these woods when our father was a little boy; and came to each of us a disquieting suspicion that perhaps they were not all gone yet, for everything seemed possible in those night-shrouded woods; and our hearts suddenly "jumped into our throats" when near by there sounded the tremulous, blood-curdling cry of the screech owl.

After about three days of gathering and boiling sap, came the "siruping down." During all that afternoon we added no more sap and we watched carefully the tawny, steaming mass in

Sugar maple growing in New Jersey

the kettle; when it threatened to boil over, we threw in a thin slice of fat pork which seemed to have some mysterious calming influence. The odor grew more and more delicious and presently the sirup was pronounced sufficiently thick. The kettle was swung off the logs and the sirup dipped through a cloth strainer into a carrying-pail. Oh, the blackness of the residue left on that strainer! But it was clean woods-dirt and never destroyed our faith in the maple-sugar, any more than did the belief that our friends were made of dirt destroy our friendship for them. The next day our interests were transferred to the house where we "sugared off." There we boiled the sirup to sugar on the stove and pouring it thick and hot upon snow made that most delicious of all sweets—the maple-wax; or we stirred it until it "grained," before we

Maple seedling

poured it into the tins to make the "cakes" of maple-sugar.

Now the old stave bucket and the sumac spile are gone; in their place the patent galvanized spile not only conducts the sap but holds in place a tin bucket carefully covered. The old caldron kettle is broken, or lies rusting in the shed. In its place, in the newfangled sugar-houses, are evaporating vats, set over furnaces with chimneys. But we may as well confess that the maple-sirup of to-day seems to us a pale and anaemic liquid, lacking the delicious flavor of the rich, dark nectar which we, with the help of cinders, smoke and various other things, brewed of yore in the open woods.

LESSON

Leading thought— The sugar maple grows very rapidly, and is therefore a useful shade tree. Its wood is used for many purposes, and from its sap is made a delicious sugar.

Method— This study of the maple should be done by the pupils out of doors, with a tree to answer the questions. The study of the leaves, blossoms and fruit may be made in the schoolroom. The maple is an excellent subject for the Tree Study lesson. The observations should begin in the fall and continue at intervals until June.

Observations—

Fall Work—

1. Where is the maple you are studying? Is it near other trees? What is the shape of the head? What is the height of the trunk below the branches? What is the height of the tree? How large around is

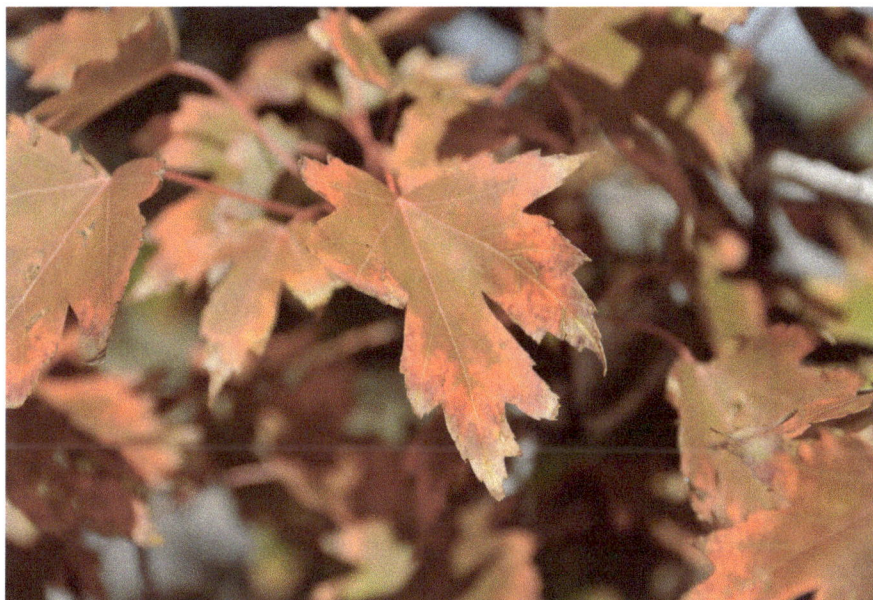

Silver maple leaves in fall

the trunk three feet from the ground? Can you find when the tree was planted? Can you tell by the shape of the tree from which direction the wind blows most often?

2. Can you find seeds on your tree? Each pair of seeds is called a key. Sketch a key, showing the way the seeds are joined and the direction of the wings. Sketch the stem which holds the key to the twig. Are both seeds of the key good or is one empty? How are the seeds scattered and planted? How far will a maple key fly on its wings? Plant a maple seed where you can watch it grow next year.

3. Make leaf prints and describe a leaf of the maple, showing its shape, its veins and petiole. Are the leaves arranged opposite or alternate on the twig? Make leaf-prints or sketches of the leaves of all the other kinds of maples which you can find. How can you tell the different kinds of maples by their leaves?

4. If your tree stands alone, measure the ground covered by its shadow from morning until evening. Mark the space by stakes. What grows beneath the tree? Do grass and other plants grow thriftily beneath the tree? Do the same plants grow there as in the open field?

5. Does your maple get its autumn colors all at once, or on one or two branches first? At what time do you see the first autumn colors on

The early stage of a maple flower

your tree? When is it completely clothed in its autumn dress? Is it all red or all yellow, or mixed? If it is yellow this year do you think it will be red next year? Watch and see. Sketch your maple in water-colors.

6. At what time do the leaves begin to fall? Do those branches which first colored brightly shed their leaves before the others? At what date does your tree stand bare?

7. Find a maple tree in the forest and compare it with one that grows as a shade tree in a field. Why this difference?

Winter Work—

8. Make a sketch of your maple with the leaves off. What sort of bark has it? Is the bark on the branches like that on the trunk? Are the main branches large? At what angle do they come off the trunk? Does the trunk extend up through the entire tree? Is the spray fine or coarse? Is it straight or crooked?

9. Study the winter buds. Are they alternate or opposite on the twigs? Are they shining or dull?

Striped maple leaves

Spring Study—

10. At what time do we tap maple trees for sap? On which side of the tree do we make the hole? If we tapped the tree earlier would we get any sap? What kind of weather is the best for causing sap flow? Do you suppose that it is the sap going up from the root to the tree and the branches, or that coming down from the branches to the root which flows into the bucket? Why do we not make maple-sugar all summer? Do you suppose the sap ceases to run because there is no more sap in the tree?

11. Write a story telling all you can find in books or that you know from your own experience about the making of maple-sugar.

12. When do the leaves of your maple first appear? How do they then look? Do they stand out or droop?

13. Do the blossoms appear with the leaves or after them? How do the blossoms look? Can you tell the blossoms with stamens from those with pistils? Do you find them in the same cluster? Do you find them on the same tree?

14. What uses do we find for maple wood? What is the character of the wood?

Supplementary reading— Trees in Prose and Poetry pp. 25-41.

The American Elm

TEACHER'S STORY

ALTHOUGH the American elm loves moist woods, it is one of those trees that enjoys gadding; and without knowing just how it has managed to do it, we can see plainly that it has planted its seeds along fence corners, and many elms now grace our fields on sites of fences long ago laid low. Because of its beautiful form and its rapid growth, the elm has been from earliest times a favorite shade tree in the Eastern and Middle States. Thirty years after being planted, the elms on the Cornell Campus clasped branches across the avenues; and the beauty of many a village and city is due chiefly to these graceful trees of bounteous shade. Moreover the elm is at no time more beautiful than when it traces its flowing lines against the background of snow and gray horizon. Whether the tree be shaped like a vase or a fountain, the trunk divides into great uplifting branches, which in turn divide into spray that oftentimes droops gracefully, as if it were made purposely to sustain from its fine tips the woven pocket-nest of the oriole. No wonder this bird so often chooses the elm for its roof-tree!

In winter, the dark, coarsely-ridged bark and the peculiar, wiry, thick spray, as well as the characteristic shape of the tree reveal to us its identity; it also has a peculiar habit of growing its short branches all the way down its trunk, making it look as if it were entwined with a vine. The elm leaf, although its ribs are straight and simple, shows a little quirk of its own in the uneven sides of its base where it joins the petiole; it is dark green and rough above, light green and somewhat rough below; but this leaf is rough only when stroked in certain directions, while the leaf of the slippery elm is rough whichever way it may be stroked. The leaf has the edges sawtoothed, which are in turn toothed; the petiole is short. The leaf comes out of the bud in the spring folded like a little fan; but before the fans are opened to the spring breezes, the elm twigs are furry with reddish green blossoms. The blossom consists of a calyx with an irregular number of lobes, and for every lobe, a stamen which consists of a threadlike filament from which hangs a bright red anther; at the center is a two-celled pistil with two light green styles. These blossoms appear in March or early April, before the leaves.

When full-grown the fruit hangs like beaded fringe from the twigs. The

Slippery elm flowers

seed is flat and has a wide, much veined margin or wing, notched at the tip and edged with a white silken fringe; the seed is at the center, wrinkled and flat. Each seed shows at its base the old calyx and is attached by a slender thread-like stem to the twig at the axils of last year's leaves. A little later the lusty breezes of spring break the frail threads and release the seeds, although few of them find places fit for growth.

The elm roots are water hunters and extend deep into the

Elm seeds

earth; they will grow towards water, seeming to know the way. The elm heart-wood is reddish, the sap-wood being broad and whitish in color; the wood is very tough because of the interlaced fibers, and therefore very hard to split. It is used for cooperage, wheel hubs, saddlery, and is now used more extensively for furniture; its grain is most ornamental. It is fairly durable as posts, but perhaps the greatest use of all for the tree is for shade. The slippery elm is much like the white elm, except that its inner bark is very mucilaginous, and children love to chew it. The cork elm has a peculiar corky growth on its branches, giving it a very unkempt look. The wahoo, or winged elm, is a small tree, and its twigs are ornamented on each side by a corky layer. The English elm has a solid, round head, very different from that of our graceful species. The elms are long-lived, some living for centuries. The Washington elm in Cambridge, and the William Penn elm in Philadelphia, which now has a monument to mark its place, were famous trees.

LESSON

Leading thought— The elm has a peculiarly graceful form, which makes it of value as a shade tree. It grows best in moist locations. Its wood is very tough.

Method— This work should be begun in the fall with the study of the shape of the tree and its foliage. Sketches should be made when the tree is clothed in autumn tints, and later it should be sketched again when its branches are naked. Its blossoms should be studied in March and April and its seeds in May.

Observations—

1. Where does the elm grow? Does it thrive where there is little water? What is the usual shape of the elm? How does the trunk divide into branches to make this shape possible? What is the shape of the larger elms? Describe the spray. Describe the elm bark. How can you tell the elm from other trees in winter?

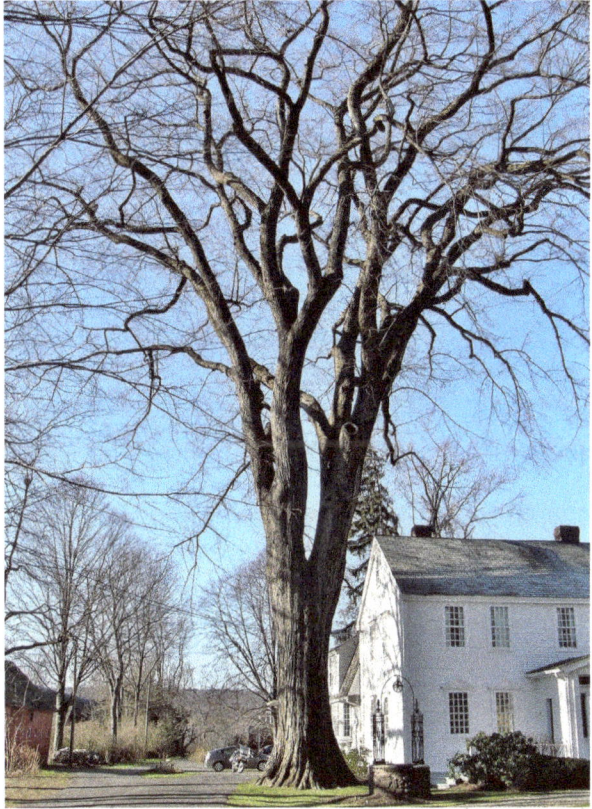

An elm in early winter

2. Study the elm leaf. What is its form? What kind of edges has it? How large is it? What is the difference in appearance and feeling between the upper and lower sides? Are the leaves rough above whichever way you stroke them? If a leaf is folded lengthwise are the two halves exactly alike? How are the leaves arranged on the twig? What is their color above and below? Describe the leafy growth along the trunk.

3. What is the color of the elm tree in autumn? Make a sketch of the elm tree you are studying.

4. What sort of roots has the elm? Do they grow deep into the earth? What is the character of its wood? Is it easy to split? Why? What are the chief uses of the elm?

5. Do you know what distinguishes the slippery elm, the cork elm, the winged elm, or wahoo, and the English elm from the common American or white elm which you have been studying?

6. Write an essay on two famous American elms.

7. What birds love to build in the elm trees?

SPRING STUDY OF THE ELM

8. Which appear first, the blossoms or the leaves? Describe the elm blossom. How long before the seeds ripen? How are the seeds attached to the twig? Describe an elm seed. How are the seeds scattered? How are the young leaves folded as they come out of the bud?

Supplementary reading— Trees in Prose and Poetry, pp. 81-92.

Flower buds emerging on a hanging elm

The beautiful fall colors of the oak tree

The Oak

TEACHER'S STORY

THE symbol of rugged strength since man first gazed upon its noble proportions, the oak more than other trees has been entangled in human myth, legend and imagination. It was regarded as the special tree of Zeus by the Greeks. Virgil sang of it thus:

"Full in the midst of his own strength he stands
Stretching his brawny arms and leafy hands,
His shade protects the plains,
His head the hills commands."

while in primitive England the strange worship of the Druids centered around it.

Although the oak is a tree of grandeur when its broad branches

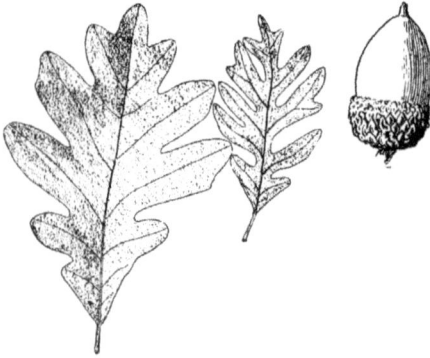

White oak leaves and acorn.

are covered with leafage, yet it is only in winter when it stands stripped like an athlete that we realize wherein its supremacy lies. Then only can we appreciate the massive trunk and the strong limbs bent and gnarled with combating the blasts of centuries. But there are oaks and oaks, and each species fights time and tempest in his own peculiar armor and in his own way. Many of the oaks achieve the height of eighty to one hundred feet. The great branches come off the sturdy trunk at wide angles, branches that may be crooked or gnarled but are ever long and strong; the smaller branches also come off at wide angles, and in turn bear angular individual spray—all of which, when covered with leaves, make the broad, rounded head which characterizes this tree. The oaks are divided into two classes which the children soon learn to distinguish, as follows:

A. *The white oak group,* the leaves of which have rounded lobes and are

White oak in winter

130

rough and light-colored below; the wood is light-colored, the acorns have sweet kernels and mature in one year, so that there are no acorns on the branches in winter. To this class belong the white, chestnut, bur, and post oaks.

AA. *The black oak group*, the leaves of which are nearly as smooth below as above, and have angular lobes ending in sharp points. The bark is dark in color, the acorns have bitter kernels and require two years for maturing, so that they may be seen on the branches in winter. To this group belong the red, scarlet, Spanish, pin, scrub, black-jack, laurel and willow oaks.

There is a great variation in the shape of the leaves on the same tree, and while the black, the red and the scarlet oaks are well-marked species, it is possible to find leaves on these

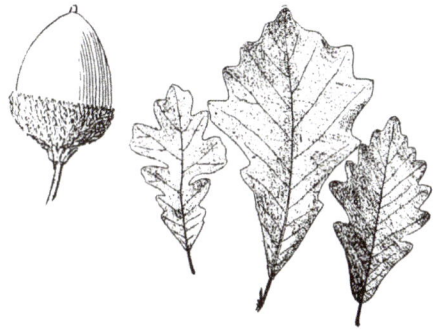

Leaves and acorn of the swamp white oak.

A swamp white oak

three different trees which are similar in shape. Oaks also hybridize, and thus their leaves are a puzzle to the botanist; but in general, the species can be determined by any of the tree books, and the pupils should learn to distinguish them.

The acorns and their scaly saucers are varied in shape, and are a delight to children as well as to pigs. The great acorns of the red oak are made into cups and saucers by the girls, and those of the scarlet oak into tops by the boys. The white oaks turn a rich wine-color in the autumn, while the bur and the chestnut are yellow. The red oak is a dark,

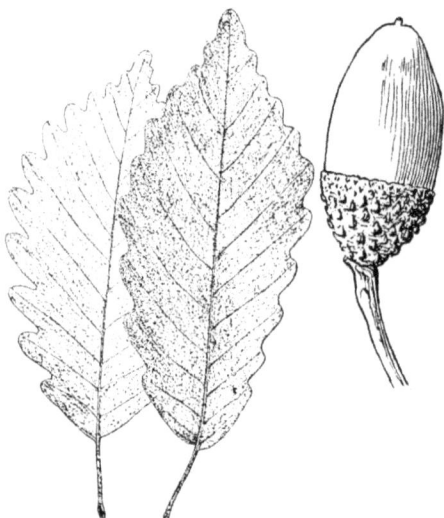
Leaves and acorn of chestnut oak.

wine-red; the black oak russet, and the scarlet a deep and brilliant red. When the oak leaves first come from the buds in the spring, they are soft and downy and drooping, those of the red and scarlet being reddish, and those of the white, pale green with red tints. Thoreau says of them, "They hang loosely, flaccidly, down at the mercy of the wind, like a new-born butterfly or dragonfly."

The pollen-bearing flowers are like beads on a string, several strings hanging down from the same point on the twig, making a fringe, and they are attractive to the eye that sees. The pistillate flowers are inconspicuous, at the axils of the leaves, and have irregular or curved stigmas; they are on the same branch as the pollen-bearing flowers.

The oak is long-lived; it does not produce acorns until about twenty years of age and requires a century to mature. Although from two to three hundred years is the average age of most oaks, yet a scarlet oak of my acquaintance is about four hundred years old, and there are oaks still living in England which were there when William, the Conqueror came. The famous Wadsworth Oak at Geneseo, N.Y. had a circumference of twenty seven feet. This was a swamp white oak. One reason for their attaining great age is long, strong, tap-roots which plant them deep, also the great number of roots near the surface which act as braces, and their large and luxurious heads.

Oak wood is usually heavy, very strong, tough and coarse. The heart is brown, the sap-wood whitish. It is used for many purposes—ships, furniture, wagons, cars, cooperage, farm implements, piles, wharves, railway ties, etc. The white and live oaks give the best wood. Oak bark is used extensively for tanning.

Leading thought— The oak tree is the symbol of strength and loyalty. Let us study it and see what qualities in it have thus distinguished it.

Method— Any oak tree may be used for this lesson; but whatever species is used, the lesson should lead to the knowledge of all the species of oaks in the neighborhood. The tree should be sketched, essays concerning the connection of the oak with human history should be written, while the leaves and acorns may be brought into the schoolroom for study. Use the leaf print lesson on page XXX for a study of leaves of all the oaks of the neighborhood.

Observations—

1. Describe the oak tree which you are studying. Where is it growing? What shape is its head? How high in proportion to the head is the trunk? What is the color and character of its bark? Describe its roots as far as you can see. Are the branches straight or crooked? Delicate or strong? Is the spray graceful or angular?

Cup and saucer made from the acorns of red oak.

2. What is the name of your oak tree? What is the color of its foliage in autumn? Find three leaves from your tree which differ most widely in form, and sketch them or make leaf prints of them for your note-book. Does the leaf have the lobes rounded, or angular and tipped with sharp points? Is the leaf smooth on the lower side or rough? Is there much difference in color between the upper and the lower side?

3. Describe the acorns which grow on your oak. Has the acorn a stem, or is it set directly on the twig? How much of the acorn does the cup cover? Are the scales on the cup fine or coarse? Is the cup rounded inwards at its rim? What is the length of the acorn including the cup? The diameter? Are there acorns on your oak in winter? If so, why? Is the kernel of the acorn sweet or bitter? Plant an acorn and watch it sprout.

4. Read all the stories you can find about oak trees, and write them in your note-book.

5. How great an age does the oak attain? Describe how the country round about looked when the oak tree you are studying was planted.

The leaves and acorn of red oak.

Leaves and acorn of black oak.

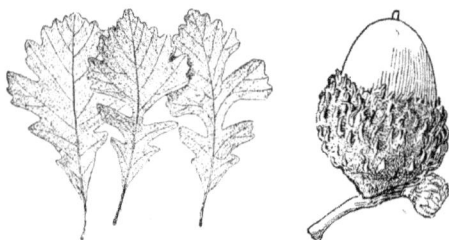

Leaves and acorn of bur oak.

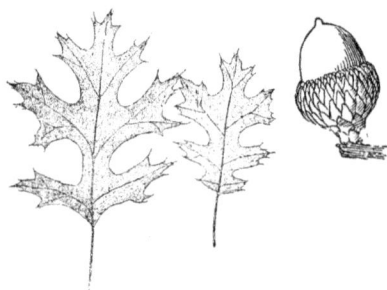

Leaves and acorn of scarlet oak.

6. How many kinds of oaks do you know? What is the difference in leaves between the white and the black oak groups? What is the difference in the length of time required for the acorns to mature in these two groups? The difference in taste of the acorns? The difference in the general color of the bark? Why is the chestnut oak an exception to this latter rule?

7. How do the oak leaves look when they first come out of the bud in spring? What is the color of the tree covered with new leaves? When does your oak blossom? Find the pollen-bearing blossoms which are hung in long, fuzzy, beady strings. Find the pistillate flower which is to form the acorn. Where is it situated in relation to the pollen-bearing flower?

8. Make a sketch of your oak tree in the fall, and another in the winter. Write the autobiography of some old oak tree in your neighborhood.

9. For what is the oak wood used? How is the bark used?

Supplementary reading— Trees in Prose and Poetry, pp. 111-129.

The Shagbark Hickory

NICHOLAS A. TONELLI
Shagbark hickory. Note loose strips of bark

HOW pathetically the untidy bark of this dignified tree suggests the careless raiment of a great man! The shagbark is so busy being something worth while that it does not seem to have time or energy to clothe itself in tailor-made bark, like the beech, the white ash and the basswood. And just as we like a great man more because of his negligence to fashion's demands, so do we esteem this noble tree, and involuntarily pay it admiring tribute as we note its trunk with the bark scaling off in long, thin plates that curve outward at the top and bottom and seem to be only slightly attached at the middle.

In general shape, the shagbark resembles the oak; the lower branches are large and, although rising as they leave the bole, their tips are deflected; and, for their whole length, they are gnarled and knotted as if to show their strength. The bark on the larger branches may be scaly toward their bases but above is remarkably smooth. The spray is angular and extends in almost every direction. The leaves, like those of other hickories, are compound. There are generally five leaflets, but sometimes only three and sometimes seven. The basal pair is smaller than the others. The hickory leaves are borne alternately on

The opening leaf bud of shagbark hickory

the twig, and from this character the hickory may be distinguished from the ashes, which have leaves of similar type, but which are placed opposite on the twigs. The shagbark usually has an unsymmetrical oblong head; the lower branches are usually shorter than the upper ones, and the latter are irregularly placed, causing gaps in the foliage.

The nut is large, with a thick, smooth, outer husk channeled at the seams and separating readily into sections; the inner shell is sharply angled and pointed and slightly flattened at the sides; the kernel is sweet. The winter buds of the shagbark are large, light brown, egg-shaped and downy; they swell greatly before they expand. There are from eight to ten bud-scales; the inner ones, which are red, increase to two or three inches in length before the leaves unfold, after which they fall away. The young branches are smooth, soft, delicate in color, and with conspicuous leaf scars.

The hickory bears its staminate and pistillate flowers on the same tree. The pollen-bearing flowers grow at the base of the season's shoots in slender, pendulous, green catkins, which occur usually in clusters of three swinging from a common stem. The pistillate flowers grow at the tips of the season's shoots singly or perhaps two or three on a common stem. In the shagbark the middle lobe of the staminate calyx is nearly twice as long as the other two, and is tipped with long bristles; it usually has four stamens with yellow anthers; its pistillate calyx is four-toothed and hairy, and has two large, fringed stigmas.

The big shagbark, or king nut, is similar to the shagbark in height, manner of growth, and bark. However, its leaves have from seven to nine leaflets, which are more oblong and wedgelike than are those of the shagbark; they are also more downy when young and remain slightly downy beneath. The nut is very large, thick-shelled, oblong, angled, and pointed at both ends. The kernel is large and sweet but inferior in flavor to the smaller shagbark. The big shagbark has larger buds than has the other. Their fringy, reddish purple, inner scales grow so large that they appear tuliplike before they fall away at the unfolding of the leaves.

Hickory wood ranks high in value; it is light-colored, close-grained, heavy, and very durable when not exposed to moisture. It is capable of resisting immense strain, and, therefore, it is used for the handles of spades, plows and other tools, and also for spokes and thills in carriage-making. As a fuel, it is superior to most woods, making a glowing, hot and quite lasting fire.

LESSON

Leading thought— The hickories are important trees commercially. They have compound leaves which are set alternately upon the twig. The shagbark can be told from the other hickories by its ragged, scaling bark.

AR ROUZ (CC BY-SA 4.0)
The fruit of a shagbark hickory

Method—This lesson may be begun in the winter when the tree can be studied carefully as to its shape and method of branching. Later, the unfolding of the leaves from the large buds should be watched, as this is a most interesting process; and a little later the blossoms may be studied. The work should be taken up again in the fall, when the fruit is ripe.

Observations—

Winter study—

1. What is the general shape of the whole tree? Are the lower branches very large? At what angle do the branches, in general, grow from the trunk? Are there many large branches?

2. Where is the spray borne? What is its character—that is, is it fine and smooth, or knotted and angled? What is its color?

3. Describe the bark. Is the bark on the limbs like that on the trunk?

4. What is the size and shape of the buds? Are the buds greenish-yellow, yellowish-brown, or do they have a reddish tinge?

5. Count the bud-scales. Are they downy or smooth?

Spring study—

6. Describe how the hickory leaf unfolds from its bud. How is each leaflet folded within the bud?

7. Describe the long greenish catkins which bear the pollen. On what part of the twigs do they grow? Do they grow singly or in clusters?

8. Take one of the tiny, pollen-bearing flowers and hold it under a lens on the point of a pin. How many lobes has the calyx? Count the stamens, and note the color of the anthers.

9. Upon what part of the twigs do the pistillate flowers grow? How many points or lobes has the pistillate calyx? Describe the growth of the nut from the flower.

Autumn study—

10. Does the hickory you are studying grow in open field or wood?

11. Are the trunk and branches slender and lofty, or sturdy and wide spreading?

12. Note the number and shape of the leaflets. Are they slim and tapering, or do they swell to the width of half their length? Are they set directly upon or are they attached by tiny stems to the mid-stem? Are they smooth or downy on the under side? Are the leaves set upon the twigs alternately or opposite each other? How are the leaflets set upon the mid-stem?

13. Describe the outer husk of the nut. Into how many sections does it open? Does it cling to the nut and fall with it to the ground? Is the nut angled and pointed, or is it roundish and without angles? Is the kernel sweet or bitter?

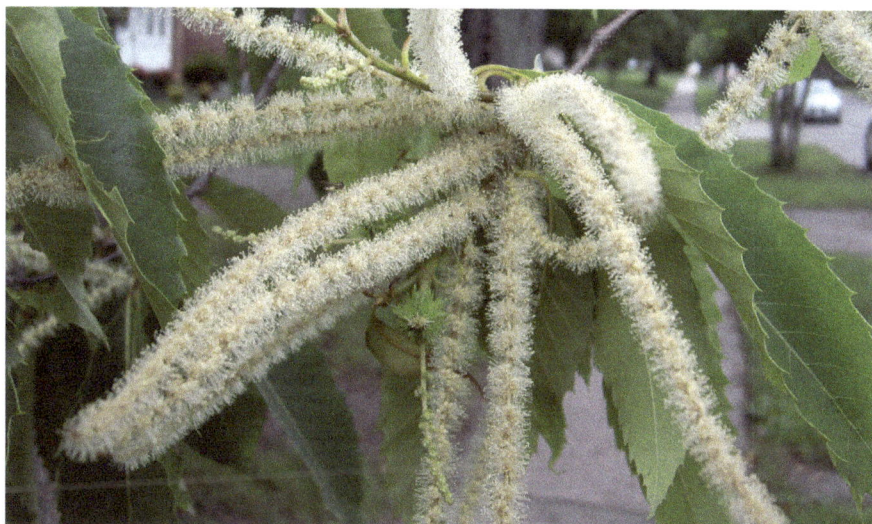

Chestnut blossom

The Chestnut

TEACHER'S STORY

THIS splendid tree, sometimes reaching the height of one hundred feet, seldom receives the admiration due to it, simply because humanity is so much more interested in food than in beauty. The fact that the chestnuts are sought so eagerly has taken away from interest in the appearance of the tree. The chestnut has a great round head set firmly on a handsome bole, which is covered with grayish brown bark divided into rather broad, flat, irregular ridges. The foliage is superb; the long, slender, graceful leaves, tapering at both ends, are glossy, brilliant green above and paler below; and they are placed near the ends of the twigs, those of the fruiting twigs seeming to be arranged in rosettes to make a background for blossom or fruit. The leaves are placed alternately and have deeply notched edges, the veins extending straight and unbroken from midrib to margin; the petiole is short. The leaf is like that of the beech, except that it is much longer and more pointed; it resembles in general shape the leaf of the chestnut

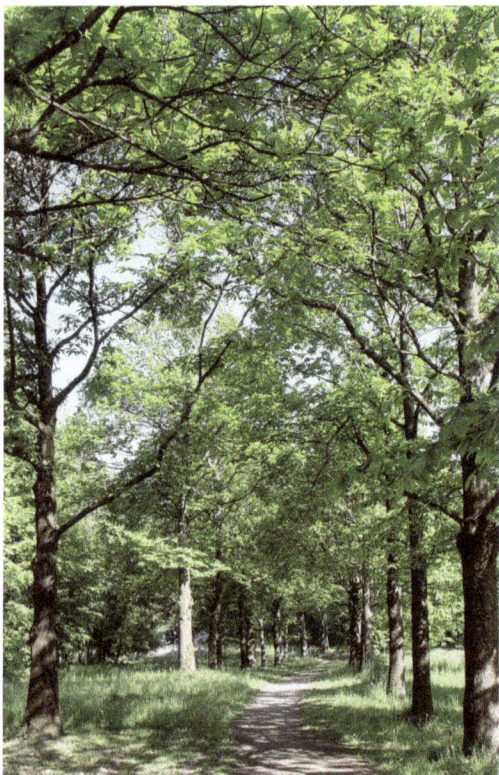

Sweet chestnut trees line a path

oak, except that the edges of the latter have rounded scallops instead of being sharply toothed. The burs appear at the axils of the leaves near the end of the twig. Thoreau has given us a most admirable description of the chestnut fruit:

"What a perfect chest the chestnut is packed in! With such wonderful care Nature has secluded and defended these nuts as if they were her most precious fruits, while diamonds are left to take care of themselves. First, it bristles all over with sharp, green prickles, some nearly a half inch long, like a hedgehog rolled into a ball; these rest on a thick, stiff, barklike rind one-sixteenth to one-eighth of an inch thick, which again is most daintily lined with a kind of silvery fur or velvet plush one-sixteenth of an inch thick, even rising into a ridge between the nuts, like the lining of a casket in which the most precious commodities are kept. At last frost comes to unlock this chest; it alone holds the true key; and then Nature drops to the rustling leaves a 'done' nut, prepared to begin a chestnut's course again. Within itself again each individual nut is lined with a reddish velvet, as if to preserve the seed from jar and injury in falling, and perchance from sudden damp and cold; and within that a thin, white skin envelops the germ. Thus, it has lining within lining and unwearied care, not to count closely, six coverings at least before you reach the contents."

The red squirrels, as if to show their spite because of the protection of this treasure chest, have the reprehensible habit of cutting off the young burs and thus robbing themselves of a rich later harvest—which serves them right. There are usually two nuts in each bur, set with flat sides together; but sometimes there are three and then the middle one is squeezed so that it has two flat sides. Occasionally there is only one nut developed in a bur—an only child, so well cared for that it grows to be almost globular. The color we call chestnut is derived from the beautiful red-brown of the polished shell of the nut, polished except where the base joins the bur, and the apex which is gray and downy.

The chestnut is always a beautiful tree, whether green in summer or glowing golden yellow in autumn; but it is most beautiful during late June and July, when covered with constellations of pale yellow stars. Each of these stars is a rosette of the pollen-bearing blossoms; each ray consists of a catkin often six

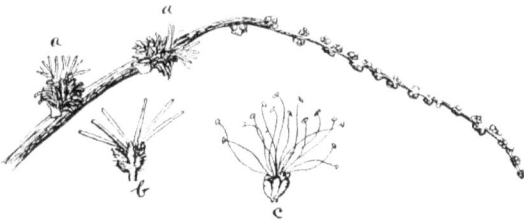

Detail of a chestnut blossom.
a, a. pistillate flowers set in a base of scales; b. pistillate flower enlarged; c. staminate flower enlarged.

or eight inches in length, looking like a thread of yellowish chenille fringe; clothing this thread in tufts for its whole length are the stamens, standing out like minute threads tipped with tiny anther balls. If we observe the blossom early enough, we can see these stamens curled up as they come forth from the tiny, pale yellow, six-lobed calyx. One calyx, although scarcely one-sixteenth of an inch across, develops from ten to twenty of these stamens; these tiny flowers are arranged in knots along the central thread of the catkin. No wonder it looks like chenille! There are often as many as thirty of these catkin rays in the star rosette; the lower ones come from the axils of the leaves; but toward the tips of the twig, the leaves are ignored and the catkins have possession. In one catkin I estimated that there were approximately 2,500 stamens developed, each anther packed with pollen. When we think that there may be thirty of the catkins in a blossom-star, we get a glimmering of the amount of pollen produced.

And what is all this pollen for? Can it be simply to fertilize the three or four inconspicuous flowers at the tip of the twig beyond and at the center of the star? These pistillate flowers are little bunches of green scales with some short, white threads projecting from their centers; and beyond them a skimpy continuation of the stem with more little green bunches scattered along it, which are undeveloped pistillate blossoms. The one or two flowers at the base of the stem get all the nourishment and the others do not develop. If we examine one of these nests of green scales, we find that there are six threads belonging to one tiny, green flower with a six-lobed calyx; the six threads are the stigmas, each one reaching out and asking for no more than one grain of the rich shower of pollen.

Chestnut wood is light, rather soft, stiff, coarse and not strong. It is used in cabinet work, cooperage, for telegraph poles and railway ties. When burned as fuel, it snaps and crackles almost equal to hemlock.

LESSON

Leading thought— The chestnut is one of our most beautiful trees. We should learn to appreciate it by observing the beauty of its blossoms and of its foliage when green and when brilliant yellow in autumn. Until the chestnut fruit is ripe, it is well protected by its spiny bur.

Method— This study may be begun in the fall when chestnuts are ripe. Ask the boys to describe the trees from which they get this longed-for harvest. The leaves, burs and nuts may be studied in the schoolroom.

Observations—

1. Where do chestnut trees grow? What is the general form of the head of the tree? How high is the trunk below the branches? Do the branches divide into fine twigs or spray at the tips?

2. Sketch and describe a chestnut leaf, showing the veins, edges and petiole. Are the leaves placed opposite or alternate? What is their color above and below? How do the chestnut leaves differ from those of the beech and of the chestnut oak? What is the color of the chestnut foliage in autumn?

3. Where on the branch is the bur borne? How does the green chest-

Chestnuts and the burr

nut bur look? Why is this prickly exterior beneficial to the fruit? Does the bur open easily when green? What causes the chestnut bur to open? Into how many lobes does it open? Describe an open bur outside and in.

4. Where in the bur are the chestnuts set? How many in one bur? How can you tell by the shape of the chestnut whether it grew as a twin or single in a bur? Are there ever three in a bur? If so, what shape is the middle one? Do the burs fall when the chestnuts are ripe?

5. Take a single chestnut. Describe its shape and color. What is the mark on its large end? Describe the coloring and covering of the tip. Open the shell and note the lining. Describe how the meat is finally protected. Can you see where the germ is? Plant a chestnut and watch it grow.

6. Study the chestnut blossom in late June or July. What kind of blossoms are those which look like yellow stars all over the tree? Study one of the catkins which makes a ray of the star, and describe it. Can you see the anthers and the pollen? How many of these pollen-bearing flowers are on one stem? Where are the pistillate flowers which will grow into young chestnuts? Describe them.

7. How much are chestnuts worth per bushel? To what uses is chestnut timber put? What is the character of the wood?

143

Horse Chestnut

The Horse-Chestnut

TEACHER'S STORY

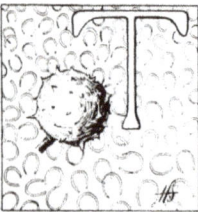

THE wealth of children is, after all, the truest wealth in this world; and the horse-chestnuts, brown and smooth, looking so appetizing and so belying their looks, have been used from time immemorial by boys as legal tender—a fit use, for these handsome nuts seem coined purposely for boys' pockets.

The horse-chestnut is a native of Asia Minor. It has also a home in the high mountains of Greece. In America, it is essentially a shade tree. Its head is a broad cone, its dark green foliage is dense and, when in blossom, the flower clusters stand out like little white pyramids against the rich back-ground in a most striking fashion. "A pyramid of green supporting a thousand pyramids of white" is a clever description of this tree's blossoming. The brown bark of the trunk has a tendency to break into plates, and the trunk is just high enough to make a fitting base for the handsome head.

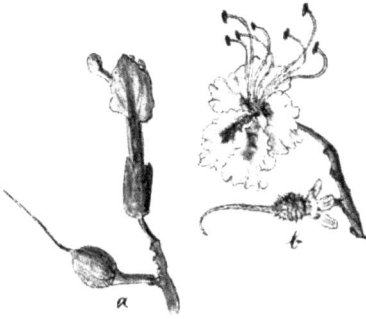

The blossom panicle is at the tip end of the twig and stops its growth at that point; the side buds continue to grow thus making a forking branch. Each blossom panicle stands erect like a candle flame, and the flowers are arranged spirally around the central stem, each pedicel carrying from four to six flowers. The calyx has five unequal lobes, and it and the stem are downy. Five spreading and unequal petals with ruffled margins are raised on short claws, to form the corolla; seven stamens with orange colored anthers are thrust far out and up from the flower. The blossoms are creamy or pinkish white and have purple or yellow blotches in their throats. Not all the flowers have perfect pistils. The stigmas ripen before the pollen, and are often thrust forth from the unopened flower. The flowers are fragrant and are eagerly visited by bumblebees, honey-bees and wasps.

Very soon after the blossom falls, there may be seen one or two green, prickly balls which are all the fruits one flower cluster could afford to mature. By October the green, spherical husk breaks open in three parts, showing its white satin lining and the roundish, shining, smooth nut at its center. At first there were six little nuts in this husk, but all except one gave up to the burly occupant. The great, round, pale scar on the nut is where it joined the husk. Very few American animals will eat the nut; the squirrels scorn it and horses surely disown it.

In winter, the horse-chestnut twig has at its tip a large bud and looks like a knobbed antenna thrust forth to test the safety of the neighborhood. There are, besides the great varnished buds at the ends of the twigs, smaller buds opposite to each other along the sides of the twig, standing out stiffly. On each side of the end bud, and below each

Horse chestnut blossoms

of the others, is a horseshoe-shaped scar left by the falling leaf of last year. The "nails" in this horseshoe are formed by the leafy fibers which joined the petiole to the twig. The great terminal buds hold both leaves and flowers. The buds in winter are brown and shining as if varnished; when they begin to swell, they open, displaying the silky gray floss which swaddles the tiny leaves. The leaves unfold rapidly and lift up their green leaflets, looking like partly opened umbrellas, and giving the tree a very downy appearance, which Lowell so well describes:

> "And gray hoss-chestnut's leetle hands unfold
> Softer'n a baby's be at three days old."

The leaf, when fully developed, has seven leaflets, of which the central ones are the larger. They are all attached around the tip of the petiole. The number of leaflets may vary from three to nine, but is usually seven. The leaflets are oval in shape, being attached to the petiole at the smaller end; their edges are irregularly toothed. The veins are large, straight and lighter in color; the upper surface is smooth and dark green, the under side is lighter in color and slightly rough. The petiole is long and shining and enlarges at both ends; when cut across, it shows a woody outer part encasing a bundle of fibers, one fiber to each leaflet. The places where these fibers were attached to the twig make the nails in the horseshoe scar. The leaves are placed opposite on the twigs.

Very different from that of the horse-chestnut is the flower of the yellow or sweet, buckeye; the calyx is tubular, long and five-lobed; the two side petals are on long stalks and are closed like spoons over the stamens and anthers; the two upper petals are also on long stalks, lifting themselves up and showing on their inner surfaces a bit of color to tell the wandering bee that here is a tube to be explored. The flowers are greenish yellow. The flowers of the Ohio buckeye show a stage between the sweet buckeye and the horse-chestnut. The Ohio buckeye is our most common native relative of the horse-chestnut. Its leaves have five leaflets instead of seven. The Sweet buckeye is also an American species and grows in the Alleghany mountains.

Lesson CXCV

Leading thought— The horse-chestnut has been introduced into America as a shade tree from Asia Minor and southern Europe. Its foliage and its flowers are both beautiful.

Method— This tree is almost always at hand for the village teacher, as it is so often used as a shade tree. Watching the leaves develop from the buds is one of the most common of the nature-study lessons. The study of the buds, leaves and fruits may be made in school; but the children should observe the tree where it grows and pay special attention to its insect visitors when it is in bloom.

Observations—

1. Describe the horse-chestnut tree when in blossom. At what time does this occur? What is there in its shape and foliage and flowers which make it a favorite shade tree? Where did it grow naturally? What relatives of the horse-chestnut are native to America?

2. Study the blossom cluster; are the flowers borne on the ends or on the sides of the twig? Describe the shape of the cluster. How are the flowers arranged on the main flower stalk to produce this form? Do the flowers open all at once from top to bottom of the cluster? Are all the flowers in the cluster the same color? Are they fragrant? What insects visit them?

3. Take a single flower; describe the form of the calyx. Is it smooth or downy? Are the lobes all the same size? Are the petals all alike in size and shape? What gives them the appearance of Japanese paper? Are any connected together? Are they all splashed with color alike?

4. How many stamens are there? Where do you see them? What color are the anthers? Search the center of a flower for a pistil with its green style. Do you find one in every flower? Could a bee reach the nectar at the base of the blossom without touching the stigma? Could she withdraw without dusting herself with pollen?

5. How long after the blossom does the young fruit appear? How does it look? How many nuts are developed from each cluster of blossoms? What is the shape of the bur? Into how many parts does it open? Describe the outside; the inside. Describe the shape of the nuts, their color and markings. Which make the best "conquerors," those which grow single in the bur or as twins? Open a nut. Can you find any division in the kernel? Is it good to eat?

Horse-chestnut Twigs and Leaves in Spring—

6. Are the buds on the twigs nearly all the same size? Where are the larger ones situated? What is the color of the buds? How are the scales arranged on them? Are they shiny or dull? What do the scales enfold? Can you tell without opening them which buds contain flowers and which ones leaves?

7. Describe the scars below the buds. What caused them? What marks are on them? What made the "nails" in the horseshoe? Has the twig other scars? How do the ring-marks show the age of the twig? Do you see the little, light colored dots scattered over the bark of the twig? What are they?

8. Describe how the leaf unfolds from the bud. What is the shape of the leaf? Do all the leaves have the same number of leaflets? Do any of them have an even number? How are the leaflets set upon the petiole? Describe the leaflets, including shape, veins, edges, color above and below. Is the petiole pliant, or stiff and strong? Is it the same shape and size throughout its length? Break a petiole, is it green throughout? What can you see at its center? Are the leaves opposite or alternate? When they fall, do they drop entire or do the leaflets fall apart from the stem?

Ohio buckeye

9. Sketch the horse-chestnut tree.

10. How do the flowers and leaves of the horse-chestnut differ from those of the sweet buckeye and of the Ohio buckeye?

Supplementary reading— Trees in Prose and Poetry, p. 17.

The Willows

They shall spring up among the grass, as willows by the water courses.
—ISAIAH.

"When I cross opposite the end of Willow Row the sun comes out and the trees are very handsome, like a rosette, pale, tawny or fawn color at base and red-yellow or orange-yellow for the upper three or four feet. This is, methinks, the brightest object in the landscape these days. Nothing so betrays the spring sun. I am aware that the sun has come out of the cloud just by seeing it light up the osiers."

—THOREAU.

THE willow, Thoreau noted, is the golden osier, a colonial dame, a descendent from the white willow of Europe. It is the most common tree planted along streams to confine them to their channels, and affords an excellent subject for a nature-study lesson. The golden osier has a short though magnificent trunk, giving off tremendous branches, which in turn branch and uphold a mass of golden terminal shoots. But there are many willows besides this, and the one who tries to determine all the species and hybrids must conclude that of making willows there is no end. The species beloved by children is the pussy willow, which is often a shrub, rarely reaching twenty feet in height. It loves moist localities, and on its branches in early spring are developed the silky, furry pussies. These are favorite objects for a nature-study lesson, and yet how little have the teachers or pupils known about these flowers!

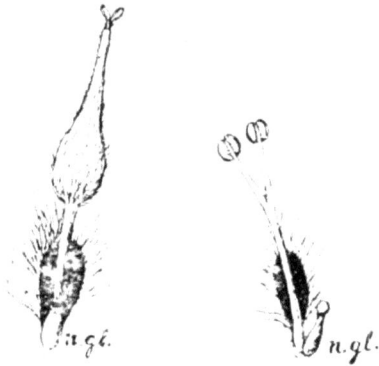

Enlarged willow blossoms.
Pistillate blossom showing nectar, gland (left);
Staminate flower showing the nectar, gland (right).

The willow pussies are the pollen-bearing flowers; they are covered in winter by a brown, varnished, double, tentlike bract. The pussy in full bloom shows beneath each fur-bordered scale two stamens with long filaments and plump anthers; but there are no pistils in this blossom. The flowers which produce seed are borne on another tree entirely and in similar greenish gray catkins, but not so soft and furry. In the pistillate catkin each fringed scale has at its base a pistil which thrusts out a Y-shaped stigma. The question of how the pollen from one gets to the pistils of another is a story which the bees can best tell. The willow flowers give the bees almost their earliest spring feast and, when they are in blossom, the happy hum of the bees working in them can be heard for some distance from the trees. The pollen gives them bee bread for their early brood, and they get their honey supply from the nectar which is produced in little jug-shaped glands, at the base of each pollen-bearing flower on the "pussy" catkin, and in a long pocket at the base of each flower on the pistillate catkin. So they pass back and forth, carrying their pollen loads to fertilize the stigmas on trees where there is no pollen. It has been asserted that the pussies, or pollen-bearing flowers, yield no nectar but give only pollen, so that the bee is obliged to seek both trees in order to secure a diet of "balanced ration;" but the person who made this statement had never taken the pains to look at the tiny jugs over-flowing with nectar found at their bases.

In June the willow seed is ripe. The catkin then is made up of tiny pods, which open like milkweed pods and are filled with seed equipped with balloons. When these fuzzy seeds are being set free people say that the willows "shed cotton."

JOHAN NEVEN

Willow pussies. The staminate blossoms of the willow

Although the seed of the willow is produced in abundance, it is hardly needed for preserving the species. Twigs which we place in water to develop flowers will also put forth roots; even if the twigs are placed in water wrong side up, rootlets will form. A twig lying flat on moist soil will push out rootlets along its entire length as though it were a root; and shoots will grow from the buds on its upper side. This habit of the willows and the fact that the roots are long, strong and fibrous make these trees of great use as soil binders. There is nothing better than a thick hedge of willows to hold streams to their proper channels during floods; the roots reach out in all directions, interlacing themselves in great masses, and thus hold the soil of the banks in place. The twigs of several of the species, notably the crack and sand-bar willows, are broken off easily by the wind and carried off down stream, and where they lodge, they take root; thus, many streams are bordered by self-planted willow hedges.

The willow foliage is fine and makes a beautiful, soft mass with delicate shadows. The leaf is long, narrow, pointed and slender, with finely toothed edges and short petiole; the exact shape of the leaf, of course,

SILK666 (CC BY-SA 3.0)
The female (left) and male (right) flowers of the pussy willow

depends upon the species, but all of them are much lighter in color below than above. The willows are, as a whole, water lovers and quick growers.

Although willow wood is soft and exceedingly light, it is very tough when seasoned and is used for many things. The wooden shoes of the European peasant, artificial limbs, willowware, and charcoal of the finest grain used in the manufacture of gunpowder, are all made from the willow wood. The toughness and flexibility of the willow twigs have given rise to many industries; baskets, hampers, carriage bodies and furniture are made of them. To get these twigs the willow trees are pollarded, or cut back every year between the fall of the leaves and the flow of the sap in the spring. This pruning results in many twigs. The use of willow twigs in basketry is ancient. The Britons fought the Roman soldiers from behind shields of basket work; and the wattled huts in which they lived were woven of willow saplings smeared with clay. Salicylic acid, used widely in medicine, is made from willow bark, which produces also tannin and some unfading dyes.

There are many insect inhabitants of the willow, but perhaps the most interesting is the little chap which makes a conelike object on the twig of certain species of willow growing along our streams. This cone is naturally considered a fruit by the ignorant, but we know that the willow seeds are grown in catkins instead of cones. This willow cone is made by a small gnat which lays its egg in the tip of the twig; as soon as the little grub hatches, it begins to gnaw the twig, and this irritation for some reason stops the growth. The leaves instead of developing along the stem are dwarfed and overlap each other. Just in the center of the cone at the tip of the twig the little larva lives its whole life surrounded by food and protected from enemies; it remains in the cone all winter, in the spring changes to a pupa, and after a time comes forth—a very delicate little fly. The larva in this gall is very hospitable. It has its own little apartment at the center but does not object to having a tenant in its outer chambers, a fact which is taken advantage of by another gall-gnat which breeds there in large numbers. It is well to gather these cones in winter; examine one by cutting it open to find the larva, and place others in a fruit jar with a cover so as to see the little flies when they shall issue in the spring.

There is another interesting winter tenant of willow leaves, but it is rather difficult to find. On the lower branches may be discovered, during winter and spring, leaves rolled lengthwise and fastened, making elongated cups. Each little cup is very full of a caterpillar which just fits it, the caterpillar's head forming the plug of the opening. This is the partially grown larva of the viceroy butterfly. It eats off the tip of the leaf each side of the midrib for about half its length, fastens the petiole fast to the twig with silk, then rolls the base of the leaf into a cup, lines it with silk and backs into it, there to remain until fresh leaves on the willow in spring afford it new food.

LESSON

Leading thought— The willows have their pollen-bearing flowers and their seed-bearing flowers on separate trees; the bees carry the pollen from one to the other. The willow pussies are the pollen-bearing flowers.

Method— As early in March as is practicable, have the pupils gather twigs of as many different kinds of willows as can be found; these should be put in jars of water and placed in a warm, sunny window. The catkins will soon begin to push out from the bud-scales, and the whole process of flowering may be watched.

Pussy willow

Observations—

1. How can you tell the common willow tree from afar? In what localities do these trees grow? What is the general shape of the big willow? How high is the trunk, or bole? What sort of bark has it? Are the main branches large or small? Do they stand out at a wide angle or lift up sharply? What color are the terminal shoots, or spray?

2. Are the buds opposite or alternate on the twigs? Is there a bud at exactly the end of any twig? How many bracts are there covering the bud?

3. Which appear first, the leaves or the blossoms? Study the pussies on your twigs and see if they are all alike. Is one kind more soft and furry than the other? Are they of different colors?

4. Take one of the furry pussies. Describe the little bract, which is like a protecting hood at its base. What color is the fur? After a few days, what color is the pussy? Why does it change from silver color to yellow? Pick one of the catkins apart and see how the fur protects the stamens.

5. Take one of the pussies which is not so furry. Can you see the little pistils with the Y-shaped stigmas set in it? Is each little pistil set at the base of a little scale with fringed edges?

6. Since the pollen-bearing catkins are on one tree and the seed-bearing catkins are on the other, and since the seeds cannot be developed without the pollen, how is the pollen carried to the pistils? For this answer, visit the willows when the pussies are all in bloom and listen. Tell what you hear. What insects do you see working on the willow blossoms? What are they after?

7. What sort of seed has the willow? How is it scattered? Do you think the wind or water has most to do with planting willow seed?

Work for May or September—

8. Describe willow foliage and leaves. How can you tell willow foliage at a distance?

9. What sort of roots has the willow? Why are the willows planted along the banks of streams? If you wished to plant some willow trees how would you do it? Would you plant seeds or twigs?

10. For what purposes is willow wood used? How are the twigs used? Why are they specially fitted for this use? What is pollarding a tree? What medicine do we get from willow bark?

11. Do you find willow cones on your willows? Cut one of these cones through and see if you can find any seeds. What is in the middle of it? What do you think made the scales of the cone? Do you think this little insect remains in here all winter?

12. In winter, hunt the lower branches of willows for leaves rolled lengthwise making a winter cradle for the young caterpillars of the viceroy.

Supplementary reading— Trees in Prose and Poetry, p. 137.

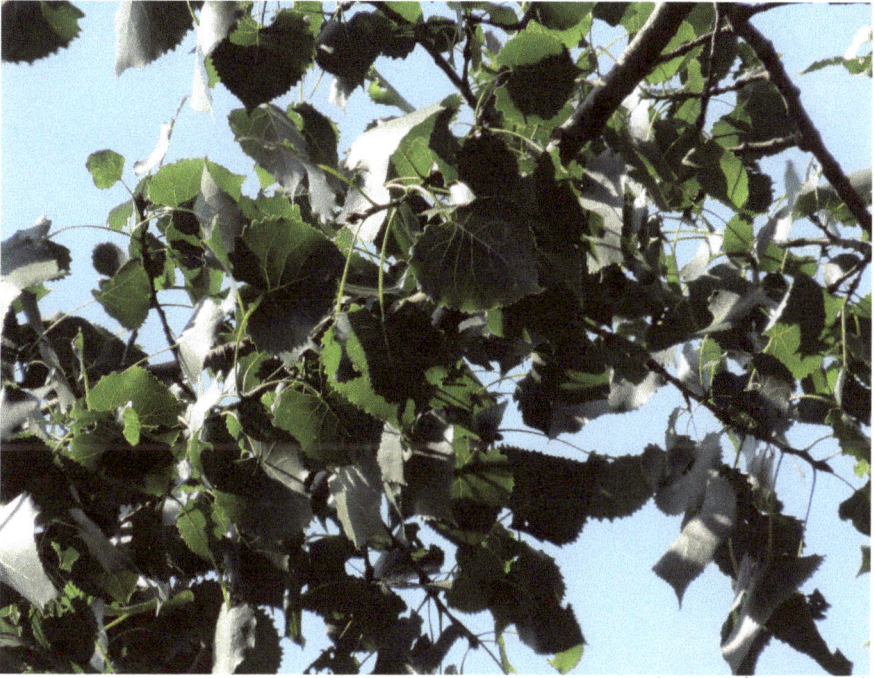

Cottonwood foliage

The Cottonwood, or Carolina Poplar

TEACHER'S STORY

THE sojourner on our western plains where streams are few and sluggish, disappearing entirely in summer, soon learns to love the cottonwoods, for they will grow and cast their shade for men and cattle where no other tree could endure. The cottonwood may be unkempt and ragged, but it is a tree, and we are grateful to it for its ability to grow in unfavorable situations. In the Middle West it attains its perfection, although in New York we have some superb specimens—trees which are more than one hundred feet in height and with majestic trunks, perhaps five or six feet through. The deep-furrowed, pale gray bark makes a handsome covering. The trunk divides into great out-swinging, widely spaced branches, which bear a fine

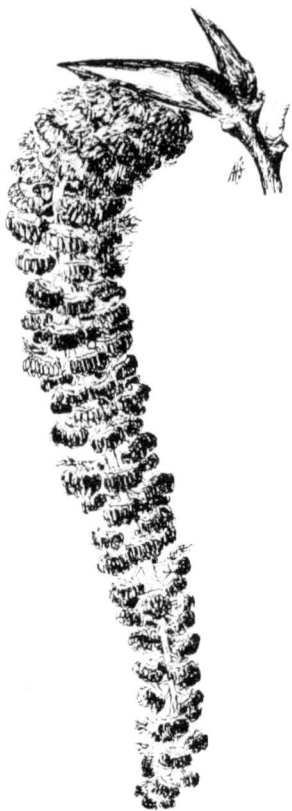
Staminate catkin of cottonwood

spray on their drooping ends. Sargent declares that at its best the cottonwood is one of the stateliest inhabitants of our eastern forests. The variety we plant in cities we call the Carolina poplar, but it is a cottonwood. It is a rapid grower, and therefore a great help to the "boom towns" of the West and to the boom suburbs in the East; although for a city tree its weak branches break too readily in wind storms in old age. However, it keeps its foliage clean, the varnished leaves shedding the dust and smoke; because of this latter quality it is of special use in towns that burn soft coal.

The cottonwood twigs which we gather for study in the spring are yellowish or reddish, those of last year's growth being smooth and round, while those showing previous growth are angular. The buds are red-brown and shining, and covered with resin which the bees like to collect for their glue. The leaf buds are slender and sharp-pointed; the flower buds are wider and plumper.

The two sexes of the flowers are borne on separate trees. The trees bearing pollen catkins are so completely covered with them that they take on a very furry, purplish appearance when in blossom. These catkins are from three to five inches long and half an inch thick, looking fat and pendulous; each fringed scale of the catkin has at its base a disc looking like a white bracket, from which hang the reddish purple anthers; these catkins fall after the pollen is shed and look like red caterpillars upon the ground.

The seed-bearing flowers are very different; they look like a string of little, greenish beads loosely strung. Each pistil is globular and set in a tiny cup, and it has three or four stigmas which are widened or lobed; as it matures, it becomes larger and darker green, and the string elongates to six or even ten inches. The little pointed pods open into two or more valves and set free the seeds, which are provided with a fluff of pappus to sail them off on the breeze; so many of the seeds develop that every object in the neighborhood is covered with their fuzz, and thus the tree has gained its name "cottonwood."

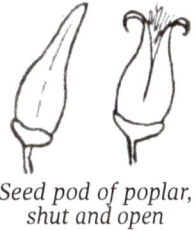
Seed pod of poplar, shut and open

The foliage of the cottonwood is like that of other poplars, trembling with the breeze. The heavy, sub-circular leaf is supported on the sidewise flattened petiole, so that the slightest breath of air sets it quaking; a gentle breeze sets the whole tree twinkling and gives the eye a fascinating impression as of leaves beckoning. The leaf is in itself pretty. It is from three to five inches long, broad, slightly angular at the base and has a long, tapering, pointed tip. The edge is saw-toothed, and also slightly ruffled except near the stem where it is smooth; it is thick and shining green above and paler beneath. The long, slender petiole is red or yellowish, and the leaves are placed alternate on the twigs.

In the autumn the leaves are brilliant yellow. The wood is soft, weak, fine-grained, whitish or yellowish, and has a satiny luster; it is not durable. It is used somewhat for building and for furniture, in some kinds of cooperage, and also for crates and woodenware; but its greatest use is for making the pulp for paper. Many newspapers and books are printed on cottonwood paper. It is common from the Middle States to the Rocky Mountains and from Manitoba to Texas.

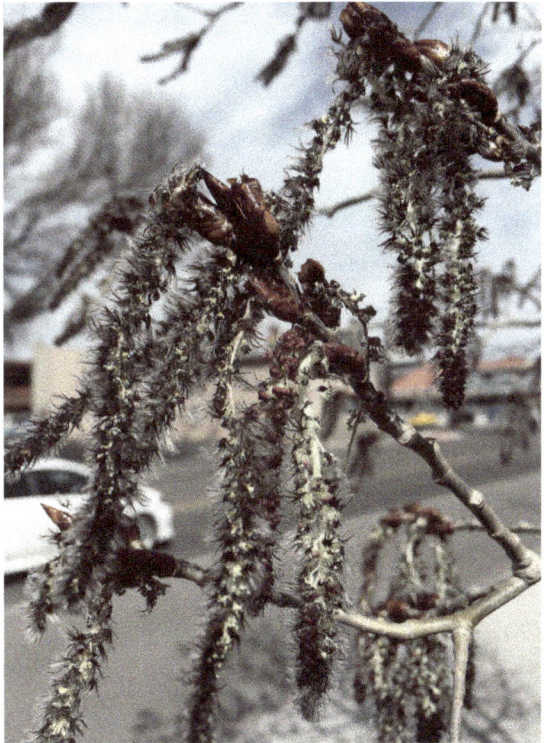
FAMARTIN (CC BY-SA 4.0)
Catkins on a trembling aspen, a near relative of the cottonwood

Cottonwood growing in the harsh conditions of New Mexico

LESSON

Leading thought— The cottonwood is a poplar. It grows rapidly and flourishes on the dry western plains where other trees fail to gain a foothold. It grows well in the dusty city, its shining leaves shedding the smoke and dirt.

Method— Begin this study in spring before the cottonwoods bloom. Bring in twigs in February, give them water and warmth, and watch the development of the catkins. Afterwards watch the unfolding of the leaves and study the tree.

Observations—

1. What is the color of the bark on the cottonwood? Is it ridged deeply? What is the color of the twigs? Are they round or angular, or both? Describe the winter buds and bud-scales. Can you tell which bud will produce leaves and which flowers?

2. Describe the catkin as it comes out. Has this catkin anthers and pollen, or will it produce seed? Do you think the seeds are produced on the same trees as the pollen?

3. Find a pollen-bearing catkin. Describe the stamens. Can you see anything but the anthers? On what are they set? What color are they?

What color do they give to the tree when they are in blossom? What happens to the catkins after their pollen is shed?

4. Find a seed-bearing catkin. How long is it? Do you see why this tree is called the necklace poplar? Describe the pistils which make the beads on the necklace.

Cottonwood seeds

5. When do the seeds ripen? If you have been near the tree, how do you know when they are ripe? How long is the catkin with the ripened seeds? How many balls on the necklace now? What is the color? How many seeds come out of each little pod? How are the seeds floated on the air? Why do we call this tree "cottonwood?"

6. How large is the largest cottonwood that you know? Sketch it to show the shape of the tree. Are the main branches large? Do they droop at the tips?

7. How does the foliage of the cottonwood look? Does it twinkle with the wind? Examine the leaves upon a branch and see why they twinkle. Are the petioles round or flat? Are they flattened sidewise or up and down? Are they stiff or slender? Describe the leaves, giving their shape, veins, edges, color and texture above and below. Are the edges ruffled as well as toothed? Is the leaf heavy? If a breeze comes along how would it affect such a heavy, broad leaf on such a slender, thin petiole? Blow against the leaves and see how they move. Do you understand, now, why they twinkle? Can you see why the leaves shed smoke and dust, when used for shading city streets?

8. Why is the cottonwood used as a shade tree? Do you think it makes a beautiful shade tree? How long does it take it to grow? What kind of wood does it produce? For what is it used?

Supplementary reading— Trees in Prose and Poetry, pp. 139-149.

The White Ash

MYTHS and legends cluster about the ash tree. It was, in the Norse mythology, the tree "Igdrasil," the tree of the universe, which was the origin of all things. It is a pity that it was not the Tree of Life in the Garden of Eden, for if another myth is true, no snake will go near it or cross its branches. There is a widespread belief that it draws lightning, just as the beech repels the thunderbolts. "As straight as a white ash tree" was the highest compliment that could be paid to the young pioneer; so straight is its fiber and so strong its quality, that the American Indians made their canoe paddles from it.

The ashes have the most beautiful bark in the world. It is divided into fine, vertical ridges, giving the trunks the look of being shaded with pencil lines; the bark smooths out on the lower branches. But even more characteristic than the bark, are the ash branches and twigs; the latter are sparse, coarse and clumsy, those of the white ash being pale or-

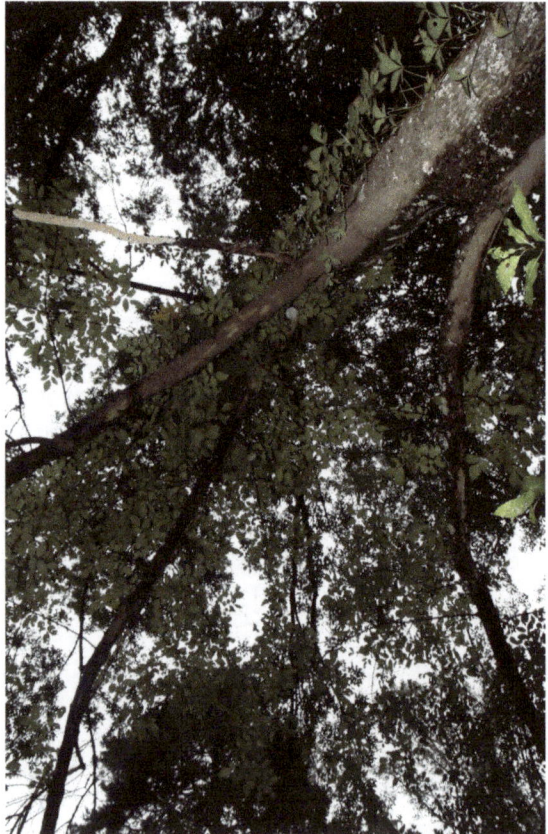

DAVID J. STANG (CC BY-SA 4.0)
An ash tree in the Botanical Gardens, Asheville N.C.

162

ange or gray and seemingly warped into curves at the ends; they are covered with whitish gray dots, which reveal themselves under the lens to be breathing-pores.

The white ash loves to grow in rich woods or in rich soil anywhere, even though it be shallow; at its best, it reaches the height of 130 feet, with a trunk six feet through. Its foliage is peculiarly graceful; the leaves are from eight to twelve inches long and are composed of from five to nine leaflets. The leaflets have little petioles connecting them with the middle stem; in shape they are ovate with edges obscurely toothed or entire; the two basal leaflets are smaller than the others and the end one largest; in texture, they are satiny, dark green above, whitish beneath, with feather-like veins, often hairy on the lower side. The petioles are swollen at the base. The leaves are set opposite upon the twig; except the horsechestnut, the ashes are our only trees with compound leaves which have the leaves opposite. This character alone readily distinguishes the ashes from the hickories. The autumn foliage has a very peculiar color; the leaves are dull purple above and pale yellow below; this brings the sunshine color into the shadowy parts of the tree, and gives a curious effect of no perspective. Notwithstanding this, the autumn coloring is a joy to the artistic eye and is very characteristic.

The seeds of the ash are borne in crowded clusters; the delicate stem, from three to five inches long, is branched into smaller stems to which are joined two or three keys, and often several of these main stems come from the same bud at the tip of last year's wood so that they seem crowded. The seed is winged, the wing being almost twice as long as the seed set at its base. Thoreau says: "The keys of the white ash cover the trees profusely, a sort of mulberry brown, an inch and a half long, and handsome." The seeds cling persistently to the tree, and I have often observed them being blown over the surface of the snow as if they were skating to a planting place.

The flowers appear in April or May, before the leaves. The pistillate flowers make an untidy fringe, curling in every direction around

GMIHAIL (CC BY-SA 3.0)
Female ash flowers

White ash bark

the twigs. The chief flower stem is three to four inches long, quite stout, pale green, and from this arise short, fringed stems, each carrying along its sides the knobs on little stems—which are the pistillate flowers. Each tiny flower seems to be bristling with individuality, standing off at its own angle to get its own pollen. The flower has the calyx four-lobed; the style is long and slender and is divided into a V-shaped purple stigma.

The staminate flowers appear early in the spring, and look like knobs on the tips of the coarse, sparse twigs; they consist of masses of thick, green anthers with very short, stout filaments; each calyx is four-lobed. These flowers are attached to a five-branching stem; but the stem and its branches cannot be seen unless the anthers are plucked off, because they hang in such a crowded mass. Later the leaves come out beyond them.

The leaf buds in winter are very pretty; they are white, bluntly pointed, with a pale gray half-circle below, on which was set last year's leaf. Another one of nature's miracles is the bouquet of leaves coming from one of the big four-parted terminal buds, which is made up of four scales, two of which are longer and narrower than the others. Within the bud each little compound leaflet is folded like a sheet of paper lengthwise, and folded with the other leaflets like the leaves of a book; and when they first appear they look like tiny, scrawny, birds' claws. But it is not merely one pair of leaves that comes from this bud, but many, each pair being set on a twig opposite and at right angles to the next pair on

White ash leaves in fall

either side. Even as many as five pairs of these splendid compound leaves come from this one prolific bud. As they push out, the green stem of the new wood grows, thus spacing the pairs properly for the making of beautiful foliage.

LESSON

Leading thought— The ashes are our most valuable timber trees; the white ash is one of the most beautiful and useful of them all. It does not make forests, but it grows in them, and its wood is of great value for many things.

Method— The pupils should all see the tree where it grows. The questions should be given to them for their field note-books. The lesson should begin in the fall and be continued in the spring.

Observations—

1. What is there about the bark of the ash tree which distinguishes it from other trees? Where does the white ash grow? What is the height and thickness of the ash tree you are studying?

2. The ash leaf is a compound leaf; of how many leaflets is it composed? What is the texture and shape of the leaflets? Describe the

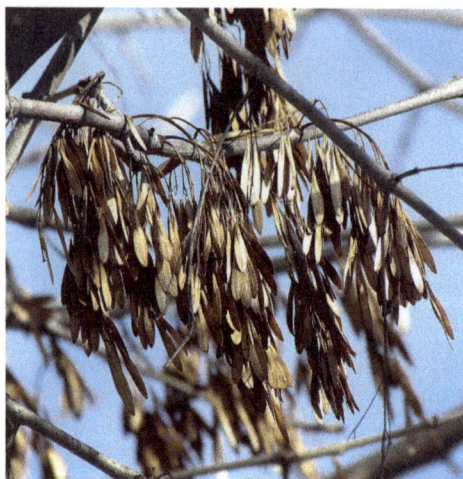
White ash seeds

veins. Do the leaflets have petioles (petiolules)? Are the edges of the leaflets toothed? Which of the leaflets is largest? Which smallest? Is the petiole swollen at the base? How are the leaves arranged on the twigs? How does this distinguish the ashes from all other of our trees having compound leaves? How do the hickories have their leaves arranged? What color is the ash foliage in autumn?

3. Describe the seeds of the ash and the way they are arranged on their stems. Where are they placed on the tree? How long do they cling? How does the snow help to scatter them?

4. When does the white ash blossom? Are the pistillate and staminate flowers together or separate? Find and describe them.

5. What are our uses for ash timber? For what are the saplings used? How did the Indians use the white ash? Write a theme on all the interesting things you can find about the ash trees.

6. How many species of the ash trees do you know?

Supplementary reading— Trees in Prose and Poetry, pp. 60-71.

> "I care not how men trace their ancestry,
> To ape or Adam; let them please their whim;
> But I in June am midway to believe
> A tree among my far progenitors,
> Such sympathy is mine with all the race,
> Such mutual recognition vaguely sweet
> There is between us. Surely there are times
> When they consent to own me of their kin,
> And condescend to me and call me cousin,
> Murmuring faint lullabies of eldest time,
> Forgotten, and yet dumbly felt with thrills
> Moving the lips, though fruitless of the words."

—From "Under the Willows," Lowell.

The Apple Tree

As the apple tree among the trees of the wood, so is my beloved among the sons. I sat down under his shadow with great delight, and his fruit was sweet to my taste.

—THE SONG OF SOLOMON.

 N old-fashioned orchard is always a delight to those of us who love the picturesque. The venerable apple tree with its great twisted and gnarled branches, rearing aloft its rounded head, and casting its shadow on the green turf below, is a picture well worthy of the artist's brush. And that is the kind of orchard I should always have, because it suits me, just as it does bluebirds, downies and chickadees, as a place to live in. However, if I wished to make money by selling apples, I should need to have an orchard of comparatively young trees, which should be straight and

An apple tree in winter

well pruned, and the ground beneath them well cultivated; for there is no plant that responds more generously to cultivation than does the apple tree. In such an orchard, a few annual crops might be grown while the trees were young, and each year there should be planted in August or September the seed of crimson clover or of some other good cover-crop. This would grow so as to protect the ground from washing during the heavy rains and thaws of fall and winter, and in the spring it would be plowed under to add more humus to the soil.

The apple originally came from southwestern Asia and the neighboring parts of Europe, but it has been cultivated so long that we have no accounts of how it began. The prehistoric lake-dwellers of Switzerland ate this fruit. In this country the apple thrives best on clay loam, although it grows on a great variety of soils; where wheat and corn grow, there will the apple also grow. In general, the shape of the apple tree head is rounded or broadly pyramidal; however, this differs somewhat with varieties. The trunk is short and rather stocky, the bark is a beautiful soft gray and is decidedly scaly, flaking off in pieces which are more or less quadrangular. The wood is very fine-grained and heavy. On this account for many years it was used for wood-engraving and is also a favorite wood for woodcarving; it makes a most excellent fuel.

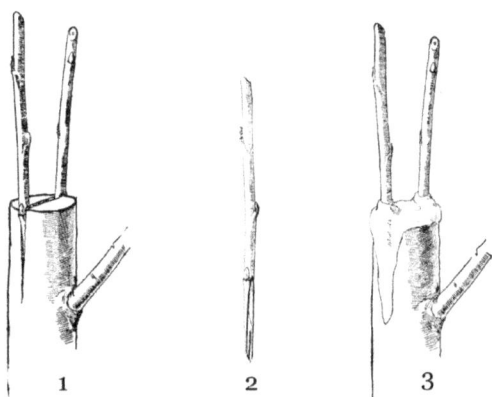

Cleft grafting
1. Cleft-graft; 2, scion for cleft-grafting,; 3, the graft waxed

The spray is fine, and while at the tips of the limbs it may be drooping or horizontal, it often grows erect along the upper sides of the limbs, each shoot looking as if it were determined to be a tree in itself. The leaves are oval, with toothed edges and long petioles. When the leaves first appear each has two stipules at its base. The shape of the apple leaves depends to some extent upon the variety of the apple.

It has long been the practice not to depend upon the seeds for reproducing a variety; for, since the bees do such a large work in pollenating the apple flowers, it would be quite difficult to be sure that a seed would not be a result of a cross between two varieties. Therefore, the matter is made certain by the process of grafting or budding. There are several modes of grafting, but perhaps the one in most common use is the cleft-graft. A scion, which is a twig bearing several buds, is cut from a tree of the desired variety, and its lower end is cut wedge-shaped. The branch of the tree to be grafted is cut off across and split down through the end to the depth of about two inches; the wedge-shaped end of the scion is pressed into this cleft, so that its bark will come in contact with the inner edge of the bark on one side of the cleft branch. The reason for this is that the growing part of the tree is the cambium layer, which is just inside of the bark, and if the cambium of the scion does not come in contact with the cambium of the branch they will not grow together. After the graft becomes well-established, the other branches of the tree are cut off and the tree produces apples only from that part of it which grows from the graft. After the scion has been set in the stock, all of the wounded parts are covered with grafting wax, which keeps in the moisture and keeps out disease germs.

Budding is done on a similar principle, but in a different fashion. A seedling apple tree about a year and a half old has a T-shaped slit

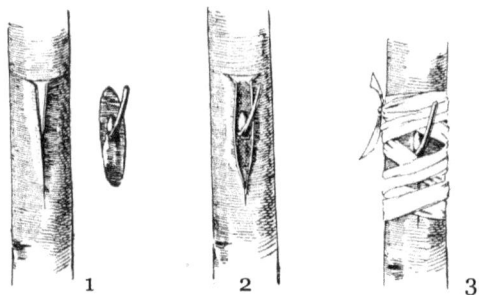

Shield-budding
1, The T-shaped slit and the bud; 2, the bud set in the slit; 3, the bud tied

cut into its bark; into this suture a bud, cut from a tree of the desired variety, is inserted, and is bound in with yarn. The next spring this tree is cut back to just above the place where the bud was set in, and this bud-shoot grows several feet; the next year the tree may be sold to the orchardist. Budding is done on a large scale in the nurseries, for it is by this method that the different varieties are placed on the market.

Most varieties of apple trees should be set forty feet apart each way. It is possible, if done judiciously, to raise some small crops on the land with the young orchard, but care should be taken that they do not rob the trees of their rightful food. The dwarf varieties begin to bear much sooner than the others, but an orchard does not come into full bearing until after it has been planted fifteen or twenty years. The present practice is to prune a tree so that the trunk shall be very short. This makes the picking of the fruit much easier and also exposes the tree less to wind and sun-scald.

There are certain underlying principles of pruning that every child should know: The pruning of the root cuts down the amount of food which the tree is able to get from the soil. The pruning of the top throws the food into the branches which are left and makes them more vigorous. If the buds at the tips of the twigs are pruned off, the food is forced into the side buds and into the fruit, which make greater growth. Thinning the branches allows more light to reach down into the tree, and gives greater vigor to the branches which are left. A limb should be pruned off smoothly where it joins the larger limb, and there should be no stump projecting; the wound should be painted so as not to allow fungus spores to enter.

We should not forget that we have a native apple, which we know as the thornapple. Its low, broad head in winter makes a picturesque point along the fences; its fine, thick spray, spread horizontally, makes a fit framework for the bridal bouquet which will grow upon it in June;

A thorn apple tree

and it is scarcely less beautiful in autumn, when covered with the little, red apples called "haws." Though we may refrain from eating these native apples, which consist of a bit of sweet pulp around large seeds, the codling-moth finds them most acceptable.

LESSON

Leading thought— The tree of each variety of apple has its own characteristic shape, although all apple trees belong to one general type. The variety of the apple grown upon the tree is not determined by the kind of seed which is planted to produce the tree, but by the process of grafting or budding the young tree.

Method— A visit to a large, well-grown orchard in spring or autumn will aid in making this work interesting. Any apple tree near at hand may be used for the lesson.

Observations—

1. How tall is the largest apple tree you know? What variety is it? How old is it? How can you distinguish old apple trees from young ones at a glance?

2. Choose a tree for study: How thick is its trunk? What is the shape of its head? Does the trunk divide into large branches or does it extend up through the center of the head?

3. What sort of bark has it? What is the color of the bark?

4. Does the spray stand erect or is it gnarled and querly? Does the spray grow simply at the ends of the branches or along the sides of the branches?

5. Are the leaves borne at the tip of the spray? Are the leaves opposite or alternate? Describe or sketch an apple leaf. Does it have stipules at its base when it first appears?

6. What is the character of apple-tree wood? What is it used for?

7. Did this tree come from a seed borne in an apple of the same variety which it produces? What is the purpose of grafting a tree? What is a scion? How and why do we choose a scion? How do we prepare a branch to receive the scion? If you should place the scion at the center of the branch would it grow? Where must it be placed in order to grow? How do we protect the cut-end of the branch after it is grafted? Why?

8. What is meant by the term "budding?" What is the difference between grafting and budding? Describe the process of budding.

9. Where is budding done on a large scale? How do nurserymen know what special varieties of apples their nursery stock will bear? How old is a tree when it is budded? How old when it is sold to the orchardist?

10. Why should the soil around apple trees be tilled? Is this the practice in the best-paying orchards?

11. What is often used as a cover crop in orchards? When is this planted? For what purpose?

12. How far apart should apple trees be set? How may the land be utilized while the trees are growing? How old must the apple tree be to come into bearing?

13. Is the practice now to allow an apple tree to grow tall? Why is an apple tree with a short trunk better?

14. What does it do to a tree to prune its roots? What does it do to a tree to prune its branches?

15. How does it affect a tree to prune the buds at the tips of the twigs?

16. How does it affect a tree to thin the branches? Describe how a limb should be pruned and how the wound thus made should be treated. Why?

A bee visiting an apple flower

How an Apple Grows

An apple tree in full blossom is a beautiful sight. If we try to analyze its beauty we find that on the tip of each twig there is a cluster of blossoms, and set around them, as in a conventional bouquet, are the pale, soft, downy leaves. These leaves and blossoms come from the terminal winter buds, which are protected during winter by little scales which are more or less downy. With the bursting of the bud, these scales fall off, each one leaving its mark crosswise on the twig, marking the end of the year's growth; these little ridges close together and in groups mark the winters which the twig has experienced, and thus reveal its age.

There is a difference in varieties of apples and in the season as to whether the blossoms or the leaves push out first. The white, downy leaves at first have two narrow stipules at the base of their petioles. They are soft, whitish and fuzzy, as are also the flower stem and the calyx, which holds fast in its slender, pointed lobes the globular flower bud. We speak of the lobes of the calyx because they are joined at the

Peach blossoms

base, and are not entirely separate as are sepals. The basal part of the calyx is cup-shaped, and upon its rim are set the large, oval petals, each narrowing to a slender stem at its base. The petals are set between the sepals or lobes of the calyx, the latter appearing as a beautiful, pale green, five-pointed star at the bottom of the flower. The petals are pink on the outside and white on the inside, and are veined from base to edge like a leaf; they are crumpled more than are the cherry petals.

The many pale, greenish white stamens of different lengths and heights stand up like a column at the center of the flower. They are tipped with pale yellow anthers, and are attached to the rim of the calyx-cup. They are really attached in ten different groups but this is not easy to see.

The five pale green styles are very silky and downy and are tipped with green stigmas. The pistils all unite at their bases making a five-lobed, compound ovary. The upper part of this ovary may be seen above the calyx-cup, but the lower portion is grown fast to it and is hidden within it. The calyx-cup is what develops into the pulp of the apple, and each of these pistils becomes one of the five cells in the apple core. If one of the stigmas does not receive pollen, its ovary will develop no seed; this often makes the apple lop-sided. When the petals first fall, the calyx-lobes are spread wide apart; later they close in toward the center, making a tube. To note exactly the time of this change is important, since the time of spraying for the codling moth is before the calyx-lobes close. These lobes may be seen in any ripe apple as five little, wrinkled scales at the blossom end; within them may be seen the dried and wrinkled stamens, and within the circle of stamens, the sere and blackened styles.

There may be five or six, or even more blossoms developed from one winter bud, and there may be as many leaves encircling them, forming a bouquet at the tip of the twig. However, rarely more than two of these blossoms develop into fruit, and the fruit is much better when only one blossom of the bouquet produces an apple; if a tree bears too many apples it cannot perfect them.

The blossoms and fruit are always at the end of the twigs and spurs of the apple tree, and do not grow along the sides of the branches

Pear blossoms

as do the cherry and the peach. However, there are many buds which produce only leaves; and just at the side and below the spur, where the apple is borne, a bud is developed, which pushes on and continues the growth of the twig, and will in turn be a spur and bear blossoms the following year.

LESSON

Leading thought— The purpose of the apple blossom is to produce apples which shall contain seeds to grow into more apple trees.

Method— This lesson should begin with the apple blossoms in the spring and should continue, with occasional observations, until the apples are well grown. If this is not possible, the blossom may be studied, and directly afterward, the apple may be observed carefully, noting its relation to the blossom.

THE APPLE BLOSSOM

Observations—

1. How are the apple buds protected in the winter? As the buds open what becomes of the protecting scales? Can you see the scars left by the scales after they have fallen? How does this help us to tell the age of a twig or branch?

2. As the winter buds open, which appear first—the flowers or the leaves? Do they both come from the same bud? Do all the buds produce both flowers and leaves?

3. Study the bud of the apple blossom. Describe its stem; its stip-

ules; its calyx. What is the shape and position of the lobes, or sepals, of the calyx? Why do we usually call them the "lobes of the calyx" instead of sepals?

4. Sketch or describe an open apple blossom. How many petals? What is their shape and arrangement? Can you see the calyx-lobes between the petals as you look down into the blossom? What sort of a figure do they make? Are the petals usually cup-shaped? What is their color outside and inside? Why do the buds seem so pink and the blossoms so white?

5. How many stamens are there? Are they all of the same length? What is the color of the filaments and anthers? On what are they set?

6. How many pistils do you see? How many stigmas are there? Are the ovaries united? Are they attached to the calyx?

7. Describe the young leaves as they appear around the blossoms. What is their color? Have they any stipules? Why do they make the flowers look like a bouquet?

8. After the petals fall, what of the blossom remains? What part develops into the apple? Does this part enclose the ovaries of the pistils? How can you tell in the ripe apple if any stigma failed to receive pollen?

9. What is the position of the calyx-lobes directly after the petals fall? Do they change later? How does this affect spraying for the codling moth?

10. Watch an apple develop; look at it once a week and tell what parts of the blossom remain with the apple.

11. How many blossoms come from one winter bud? How many leaves? Do the blossoms ever appear along the sides of the branches, as in the cherries? How many blossoms from a single bud develop into apples?

12. Since the apple is developed on the tip of the twig how does the twig keep on growing?

13. Compare the apple with the pear, the plum, the cherry and the peach in the following particulars: position on the twigs; number of petals; number and color of stamens; number of pistils; whether the pistils are attached to the calyx-cup at the base.

The Apple

TEACHER'S STORY

"Man fell with apples and with apples rose,
If this be true; for we must deem the mode
In which Sir Isaac Newton could disclose,
Through the then unpaved stars, the turnpike road,
A thing to counterbalance human woes."

—BYRON.

APPLES seem to have played a very important part in human history, and from the first had much effect upon human destiny, judging from the trouble that ensued both to Adam and to Helen of Troy from meddling, even though indirectly, with this much esteemed fruit. It is surely no more than just to humanity—shut out from the Garden of Eden—that the apple should have led Sir Isaac Newton to discover the law which holds us in the universe; and that, in these later centuries, apples have been developed, so beautiful and so luscious as almost to reconcile us to the closing of the gates of Paradise.

While it is true that no two apples were ever exactly alike, any more than any two leaves, yet their shapes are often very characteristic of the varieties. From the big, round Baldwin to the cone-shaped gilly-flower, each has its own peculiar form, and also its own colors and markings and its own texture and flavor. Some have tough skins, others bruise readily even with careful handling; but to all kinds, the skin is an armor against those ever-present foes, the fungus spores, myriads of which are floating in the air ready to enter the smallest breach, and by their growth bring about decay. Even the tip of a branch or twig swayed by the wind, may bruise an apple and cause it to rot; windfalls are always bruised and will not keep. Greater care in packing, wrapping, picking and storing, so as to avoid contact with other apples, is a paying investment of labor to the apple grower.

The cavities at the stem and basin-ends of the fruit are also likely to have, in the same variety, a likeness in their depth or shallowness, and thus prove a help in identifying an apple. At the blossom, or basin, end of the fruit may be seen five scales, which are all that remain of the calyx-lobes which enclosed the blossom; and within them are the withered and shrunken stamens and styles.

When the fruit is cut, we see that the inner parts differ as much in the different varieties as do the outer parts. Some have large cores,

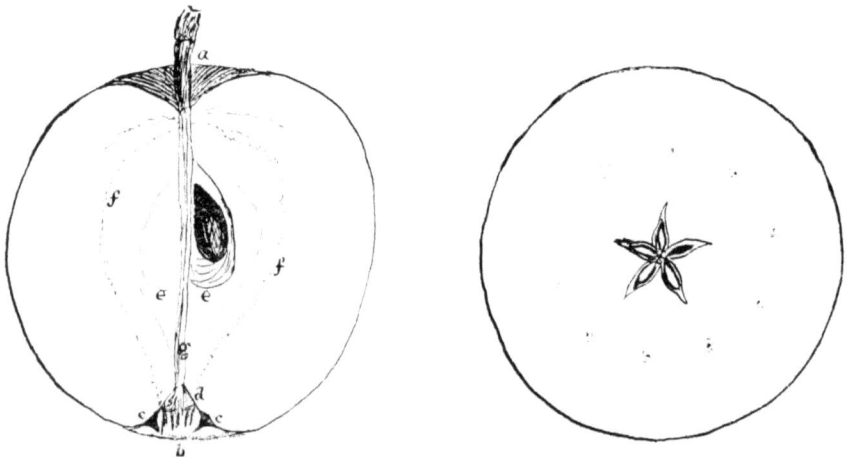

a, cavity; b, basin; c, calyx lobes; d, calyx tube with the withered stamens attached; e, carpels; f, outer core-lines, terminating at a point where stamens are attached; g, fibres extending from stem to basin. Transverse section of apple showing the five carpels and the ten outer core-lines.

others small. The carpels, or seed-cells, are five in number, and when the fruit is cut across through the center these carpels show as a pretty, five-pointed star; in them the seeds lie, all pointing toward the stem. Some apples have both seeds and carpels smooth and shining, while in others they are tufted with a soft, fuzzy outgrowth. The number of seeds in each cell varies; the usual number is two. In case a carpel is empty, the apple is often lopsided, and this signifies that the stigma of that ovary received no pollen. The apple seed is oval, plump and pointed, with an outer shell, and a delicate inner skin covering the white meat; this separates readily into two parts, between which, at the point, may be seen the germ. The entire core, with the pulp immediately surrounding the seed cells, is marked off from the rest of the pulp by the core-lines, faint in some varieties but distinct in others. In our native crab-apples this separation is so complete that, when the fruit is ripe, the core may be plucked out leaving a globular cavity at the center of the apple.

Extending from the stem to the basin, through the center of the apple, is a bundle of fibers, five in number, each attached to the inner edge of a carpel, or seed-box. Other bundles of fibers pass through the flesh about half way between the core and the skin. Delicate as they are, so that no one observes them in eating the fruit, they show clearly as a second core-line, and each terminates at a point in the calyx-tube where the stamens were attached—as can be easily seen by dissecting an apple. In transverse section, these show as

Wild apples

ten faint dots placed opposite each outer point and inner angle of the star at the center formed by the carpels. Sometimes the seed-cells are very close to the stem, and the apple is said to have a sessile core; if at the center of the fruit, it has a medium core; if nearest to the blossom end, it has a distant core. This position of the core marks different varieties.

A basket of apples

Apples even of the same variety, differ much in yield and quality according to the soil and climate in which they grow. The snow apple grows best in the St. Lawrence Valley, and New York State is noted for the fine flavor of the Esopus spitzenburg, the northern spy, and the Newtown pippin, all of which originated and grow best within its boundaries. Thus, each locality has its favorite variety.

Too often in passing through the country, we see neglected and unprofitable orchards, with soil untilled, the trees unpruned and scale-infested, yielding scanty fruit, fit only for the cider mill and the vinegar barrel. This kind of orchard must pass away and give place to the new horticulture.

References— Popular Apple Growing, Green; *The American Apple Orchard*, Waugh; *The Apple and How to Grow It*, Farmers' Bulletin 113, U. S. Department of Agriculture.

LESSON

Leading thought— The apple is a nutritious fruit, wholesome and easily digested. The varieties of apple differ in shape, size, color, texture and flavor. A perfect apple has no bruise upon it and no worm-holes in it.

Method— Typical blossoms of different varieties of apples should be brought into the schoolroom, where the pupils may closely observe and make notes about their appearance. Each pupil should have one or two apples that may be cut in vertical and transverse sections, so that the pulp, core-lines, carpels and seeds may be observed. After this lesson there should be an apple exhibit, and the pupils should be taught how to score the apples according to size, shape, color, flavor and texture.

Observations—

1. Sketch the shape of your apple. Is it almost spherical, or flattened, or long and egg-shaped, or with unequal tapering sides? How does the shape of the apple help in determining its variety?

2. What is the color of the skin? Is it varied by streaks, freckles or blotches? Has it one blushing cheek the rest being of a different color?

3. Is the stem thick and fleshy, or short and knobby, or slender and woody and long? Does each variety have a characteristic stem?

4. Is the cavity or depression where the stem grew narrow and deep like a tunnel, or shallow like a saucer?

5. Examine the blossom end, or basin. What is its shape? Can you find within it the remnants of the calyx-lobes, the stamens and the pistils of the flower?

6. What is the texture of the skin of the apple? Is it thin, tough, waxy or oily? Has it a bloom that may be rubbed off? From what sort of injury does the skin protect the apple?

Experiment 1. Take three apples of equal soundness and peel one of them; place them on a shelf. Place one of the unpeeled apples against the peeled one, and the other a little distance from it. Does the peeled apple begin to rot before the other two? Does the unpeeled apple touching the peeled one begin to decay first at the point of contact?

Experiment 2. Take an apple with a smooth, unblemished skin and vaccinate it with some juice from an apple that has begun to decay; perform the operation with a pin or needle, pricking first the unsound fruit and then the sound one; this may be done in patterns around the apple or with the initials of the operator's name. Where does this apple begin to decay? What should these two experiments teach us as to the care and storage of fruit?

7. Cut an apple through its center from stem to blossom end. Describe the color, texture and taste of the pulp. Is it coarse or fine-grained? Crisp or smooth? Juicy, or dry and mealy? Sweet or sour? Does it exhale a fragrance or have a spicy flavor?

8. Is the flesh immediately surrounding the core separated from the rest of the pulp by a line more or less distinct? This is called the core-line and differs in size and outline in different varieties. Can you find any connection between the stem and blossom ends and the core? Can you see the fibrous threads which connect them?

9. Cut an apple transversely across the middle. In what shape are the seed-cells arranged in the center? Do the carpels, or seed-cells, vary in shape in different varieties? Are they closed, or do they all open into a common cavity? Can you see, between the core-lines and the skin, faint little dots? Count, and tell how they are arranged in relation to the star formed by the core.

10. The stiff, parchment-like walls of the seed-cells are called carpels. How many of these does the apple contain? Do all apples have the same number of carpels? Are the carpels of all varieties smooth and glossy, or velvety? How many seeds do you find in a carpel? Do they lie with the points toward the stem-end or the blossom-end of the apple? Where are they attached to the apple? Describe the apple seed—its outer and inner coat and its "meat." Can you find the germ within it which will, after the seed is planted, produce another apple tree?

11. Is the core at the center of the apple, or is it nearer to the stem-end or to the blossom-end of the fruit? Are all apples alike in this particular?

12. Describe fully all the varieties of apples which you know, giving the average size, texture and color of the skin, the shape of the cavities at the stem and blossom ends, the color, texture and flavor of the pulp, and the position within the apple of the core.

Supplementary reading— Trees in Prose and Poetry, pp. 43-59.

Pine trees in winter

The Pine

TEACHER'S STORY

NONE other of our native trees is more beautiful than the pine. In the East, we have the white pine with its fine-tasselled foliage, growing often 150 to 200 feet in height and reaching an age of from two to three hundred years. On the Pacific coast, the splendid sugar pine lifts its straight trunk from two to three hundred feet in height; and although the trunk may be from six to ten feet in diameter yet it looks slender, so tall is the tree. A sugar pine cone on my desk measures 22 inches in length and weighs almost one pound, although it is dried and emptied of seed.

There is something majestic about the pines, which even the most ignorant feel. Their dark foliage outlined against wintry skies appeals to the imagination, and well it may, for it represents an ancient tree-costume. The pines are among the most ancient of trees, and were the contemporaries of those plants which were put to sleep, during the

Austrian black pine cones

Devonian age, in the coal beds. It is because the pines and the other evergreens belong essentially to earlier ages, when the climate was far different than it is to-day, that they do not shed their leaves like the more recent, deciduous trees. They stand among us, representatives of an ancient race, and wrap their green foliage about them as an Indian sachem does his blanket, in calm disregard of modern fashion of attire.

All cone-bearing trees have typically a central stem from which the branches come off in whorls, but so many things have happened to the old pine trees that the evidence of the whorls is not very plain; the young trees show this method of growth clearly, the white pine having five branches in each whorl. Sometimes pines are seen which have two or three stems near the top; but this is a story of injury to the tree and its later victory.

The very tip of the central stem in the evergreens is called "the leader," because it leads the growth of the tree upward; it stretches up from the center of the whorl of last year's young branches, and there at its tip are the buds which produce this year's branches. There is a little beetle which seems possessed of evil, for it likes best of all to lay its rascally eggs in the very tip of this leader; the grub, after hatching, feeds upon the bud and bores down into the shoot, killing it. Then comes the question of which branch of the upper whorl shall be elected to rise up and take the place of the dead leader; but this is an election which we know less about than we do of those resulting from our blanket ballots. Whether the tree chooses, or whether the branches aspire, we may not know; but we do know that one branch of this upper whorl arises and continues the growth of the tree. Sometimes there are two candidates for this position, and they each make such a good struggle for the place that the tree grows on with two stems instead of one—and sometimes with even three. This evil insect injures the leaders of other conifers also, but these are less likely to allow two competitors to take the place of the dead leader.

The lower branches of many of the pines come off almost at right angles from the bole; the foliage is borne above the branches, which gives the pines a very different appearance from that of other trees. The foliage of most of the pines is dark green, looking almost black in winter; the pitch pine has the foliage yellowish green, and the white pine, bluish green; each species has its own peculiar shade. There is great variation in the color and form of the bark of different species. The white pine has nearly smooth bark on the young trees, but on the older ones it has ridges that are rather broad, flat and scaly, separated by shallow sutures, while the pitch pine has its bark in scales like the covering of a giant alligator.

The foliage of the pine consists of pine needles set in little bundles on raised points which look like little brackets along the twigs. When the pine needles are young, the bundle is enclosed in a sheath making the twig look as if it were covered with pin-feathers. In many of the species this sheath remains, encasing the base of the bundle of needles; but in the white pine it is shed early. The number of leaves in the bundle helps to determine the tree; the white pine has five needles in each bunch, the pitch pine has three, while the Austrian pine has two. There is a great difference in the length and the color of the needles of different species of pine. Those of the white pine are soft, delicate and pliable, and from three to four inches in length; the needles of the

Young pine cones

pitch pine are stiff and coarse and about the same length; the white pine needles are triangular in section, and are set so as to form distinct tassels, while those of the Austrian pine simply clothe the ends of the twigs. The needles of the pine act like the strings of an aeolian harp; and the wind, in passing through the tree, sets them into vibration, making a sighing sound which seems to the listener like the voice of the tree. Therefore, the pine is the most companionable of all our trees and, to one who observes them closely, each tree has its own tones and whispers a different story.

The appearance of the unripe cone is another convincing evidence that mathematics is the basis of the beautiful. The pattern of the overlapping scales is intricate and yet regular—to appreciate it one needs to try to sketch it. Beneath each scale, when it opens wide, we find nestled at its base two little seeds in twin boxes; each provided with a little wing so that it can sail off with the wind to find a place to grow. The shape of the scales of the cone is another distinguishing character of the pine, and sketching the outside of scales from several different species of pine cones will develop the pupils' powers of observation; the tip of the scale may be thickened or armed with a spine, and one wonders if these spines are for the purpose of discouraging the squirrels from stealing the green seeds.

The pine cone requires two years for maturing; the pistillate flower from which it is developed is a tiny cone with each scale spread wide and standing upright to catch the pollen for the tiny ovule nestled within it. The pistillate flower of the white pine grows near the tip of the new twig, and is pinkish in color. In the Austrian pine it is the merest pink dot at first, but after a little shows itself to be a true cone with pink-purple scales, which stand up very erect, and makes a pretty object when viewed through a lens; each scale is pink at its three-pointed tip, with pink

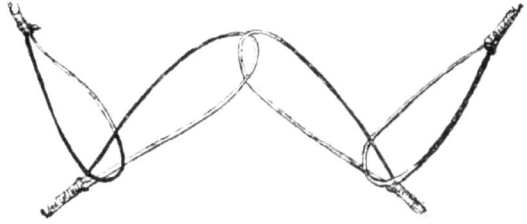

A part of a necklace of pitch pine needles

wings just below, the inner portions being pale green. The cone is set just beside the growing tip of the twig, is pointed upward, and its sheath-scales are turned back like chaff around its base.

In June when the new shoots of the pine twigs stand up like pale green candles on a Christmas tree, at their bases may be found the staminate catkins set in radiating whorls, making galaxies of golden stars against the dark green background of foliage. In the Austrian pine, one of these pollen catkins may be an inch or two long and a half-inch in width; each little scale of this cone is an anther sac, filled to bursting with yellow pollen. From these starry pollen cones there descends a yellow shower every time a breeze passes; for the pine trees depend upon the wind to sift their pollen dust into the lifted cups of the cone scales, which will close upon the treasure soon. The pollen grains of pine are very beautiful when seen through a microscope; and it seems almost incredible that the masses of yellow dust sifted in showers from the pines when in blossom, should be composed of these beautiful structures. When the pine forests on the shores of the Great Lakes are in bloom, the pollen covers the waves for miles out from the shores.

If we examine the growing tips of the pine branches, we find the leaves look callow and pin-feathery. The entire leaf is wrapped in a smooth, shining, silken sheath, at the tip of which its green point protrudes. The sheath is tough like parchment and is cylindrical because the pine needles within it are perfectly adjusted one to another in cylindrical form. The sheath is made up of several layers, one over the other, and may be pulled apart. The new leaves are borne on the new, pale green wood.

The uses of pines are many. The lumber of many of the species, especially that of the white pine, is free from knots and is used for

A mexican nut pine in Texas

almost everything from house-building to masts for ships. In the Southern States, the long-leafed pines are tapped for resin, which is not the sap of the tree, as is generally supposed. Pine sap is like other sap; the resin is a product of certain glands of the tree, and is of great use to it in closing wounds and thus keeping out the spores of destructive fungi. It is this effort of the tree to heal its wounds that makes it pour resin into the cuts made by the turpentine gatherers. This resin is taken to a distillery, where the turpentine is given off as a vapor and condensed in a coiled tube which is kept cold. What is left is known as "rosin."

LESSON

Leading thought— The pines are among our most ancient trees. Their foliage is evergreen but is shed gradually. The pollen-bearing and the seed-bearing flowers are separate on the tree. The seeds are winged and are developed in cones.

Method— At least one pine tree should be studied in the field. Any species will do but the white pine is the most interesting. The Austrian pine which is commonly planted in parks is a good subject. The leaves and cones may be studied in the schoolroom, each pupil having a specimen.

Observations—

1. What is the general shape of the pine tree? Is there one central stem running straight up through the center of the tree to the top? Do

Dozens of Lodgepole Pine male cones (orange and flower-like) occur in a cluster; the female cone is still immature (olive green).

you find any trees where this stem is divided into two or three near the top? Describe how the pine tree grows. What is the "leader?" What happens if the leader is injured? How do the topmost branches of the young pine look? Do they all come off from the same part of the stem? How many are there in a whorl?

2. What color is the bark? Is it ridged or in scales?

3. Do the branches come off the main stem at right angles or do they lift up or droop down? Where is the foliage borne on the branches? What is the color of the foliage? Is the pine foliage ever shed or does the pine leaf, when it comes, stay on as long as the tree lives?

4. Study the pine leaves. Why are they called needles? Note that they grow several together in what we call a bundle. How many in one bundle? Is the bundle enclosed in a little sheath at the base? Are the bundles grouped to make distinct tassels? Study one of the needles. How long is it? Is it straight or curved? Flexible or coarse and stiff? Cut it across and examine it with a lens. What is the outline in cross section? Why does the wind make a moaning sound in the pines?

5. Study a pine cone. Does it grow near the tip of the branch or along the sides? Does it hang down or stand out stiffly? What is its length? Sketch or describe its general shape. Note that it is made up of short, over-lapping scales. What pattern do the scales make as they

White pine cone

are set together? Describe or sketch one scale; has it a thickened tip? Is there a spine at the tip of the scale?

6. Where in the cone are the seeds? Describe or sketch a pine seed. How long is its wing? How is it carried and planted? When the cone opens, how are the seeds scattered? What creatures feed upon the pine seed?

7. Study the pine when in blossom, which is likely to occur in June. This time is easily determined because the air around the tree is then filled with the yellow pollen dust. Study the pollen-bearing flower. Is it conelike in form? Does it produce a great deal of pollen? If you have a microscope, look at the pollen through a high objective and describe it. How many of the pollen catkins are clustered together? On what part of the twigs are they borne? Where are the pistillate flowers which are to form the young cones? How large are they and how do they look at the time the pollen is flying? Do they point upward or droop downward? Why? Look beneath the scales of a little cone with a lens and see if you can find the flowers. What carries the pine pollen to the flowers in the cone?

8. Name all the uses for pine lumber that you know. Write an English theme on how turpentine is produced from pines and the effect of this industry upon pine forests. Where does resin appear on the pine? Of what use is it to the tree? Do you think it is pine sap? What is the difference between resin and rosin?

9. How long do the pine trees live? Write a story of all that has happened to your neighborhood since the pine tree which you have been studying was planted.

10. Make the following drawings: A bundle of pine needles showing the sheath and its attachment to the twig; the cone; the cone scale; the seed. Sketch a pine tree.

Supplementary reading— Trees in Prose and Poetry, pp. 32, 151, 152; The Spirit of the Pine, Bayard Taylor; To a Pine Tree, Lowell; Nature in Verse, pp. 15, 288.

The Norway Spruce

THE Norway spruce is a native of Europe, and we find it in America the most satisfactory of all spruces for ornamental planting; it lifts its slender cone from almost every park and private estate in our country, and is easily distinguished from all other evergreens by the drooping, pendant habit of its twigs, which seem to hang down from the straight, uplifted branches. We have spruces of our own—the black, the white and the red spruces; and it will add much to the interest of this lesson for the pupils to read in the tree and forestry books concerning these American species. Chewing gum and spruce beer are the products of the black and red spruce of our eastern forests. The Douglas spruce, which is a fir and not a spruce, is also commonly planted as an ornamental tree, but it is only at its best on the Pacific Coast, where it is one of the most magnificent of trees.

The Norway spruce tree is in form a beautiful cone, slanting from its slender tip to the ground, on which its low-

TIIA MONTO (CC BY-SA 3.0)
Norway spruce

191

Cones dangling on a norway spruce

er drooping branches rest; the upper branches come off at a narrower angle from the sturdy central stem than do the widespreading lower branches. On the older trees, the twigs hang like pendulous fringes from the branches, enabling them to shed the snow more readily—a peculiarity which is of much use to the tree, because it is a native of the snowy northern countries of Europe and also grows successfully in the high altitudes of the Alps and other mountains. If we stroke a spruce branch toward the tip, the hand slides smoothly over it; but brush backward from the tip, and the hand is pricked by hundreds of the sharp, bayonet-pointed leaves; this is another arrangement for letting the snow slide off.

If we examine a twig of the present year's growth, we can see on every side of its brown stem the pointed leaves, each growing from a short ridge; but the leaves on the lower side stretch out sidewise to get the light, and those above lift up angularly. Perhaps the twig of last year's growth has shed its leaves which grew on the under side and thus failed to reach the sun. The leaf of the spruce is curved, stiff, four-sided and ends in a sharp point. It is dark yellowish above and lighter beneath and is set stiffly on the twig. The winter buds for next year's growth may be seen at the tips of the twigs, covered with little, recurved, brown scales quite flowerlike in form. In the balsam fir, which is often planted with the Norway spruce, these buds are varnished.

The cones are borne on the tips of the branches and hang down. In color they are pale, wood-brown; they are from four to six inches long, and are very conspicuous. They are made up of broad scales that are thin toward the notched tips; they are set around the central stem in spirals of five rows. If we follow one spiral around marking it with a winding string, it will prove to be the fifth row above the place where we started. These manifold spirals can be seen sometimes by looking into the tip end of a cone. The cone has much resin on it, and is a very safe box for seeds; but when it begins to open, squirrels impatiently tear it to pieces, harvesting the seeds and leaving a pile of cone-scales beneath the tree to tell of their piracy.

A Norway spruce in blossom is a beautiful sight; the little, wine-red pistillate cones are lifted upwards from the tips of the twigs, while short, terminal branches are laden with the pollen-bearing catkins, which are soft and caterpillarish, growing on soft, white stems from the base of scales which enclosed and protected them during the winter; these catkins are filled with the yellow dust. The young cones continue to stand upright after the scales have closed on the pollen which has been sifted by the wind to the ovules which they guard; and for some time they remain most ornamentally purplish red. Before the cone is heavy enough to bend from its own weight, it turns deliberately around and downward, as if the act were a wilful deed, and then changes its color to green, ripening into brown in the fall.

The Norway spruce grows on the Alps abundantly, and like the youth with the banner, "excelsior" is not only its motto but its scientific name, *(Picea excelsa)*. Here it grows to the height of one hundred to one hundred and fifty feet. Its wood is valuable and its pitch is marketed. In this country, it is used chiefly for ornamental planting and for wind-breaks.

LESSON

Leading thought— The Norway spruce is one of the most valuable of the trees which have come to America from Europe. It grows natu-

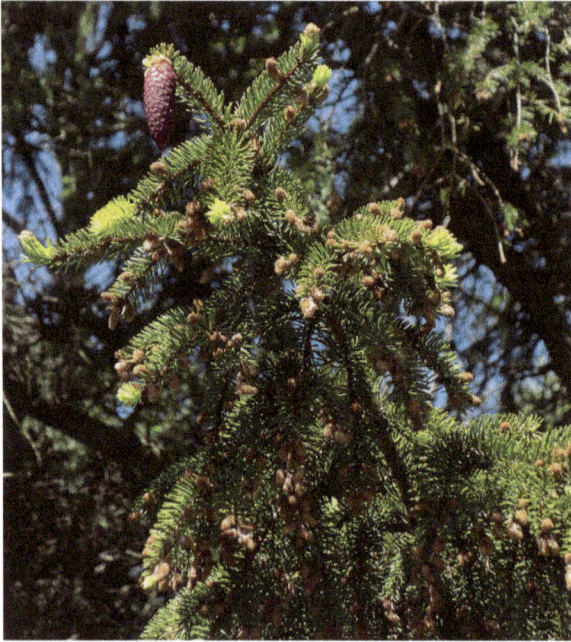
Male flowers and an immature cone on a Norway spruce

rally in high places and in northern countries where there is much snow; its drooping twigs cannot hold a great burden of snow, and thus it escapes being crushed.

Method— This lesson should begin in the autumn when the cones are ripe. The tree should be observed by all of the pupils, and they should bring in twigs and cones for study in the schoolroom. The lesson should be taken up again in May when the trees are in blossom.

Observations—

1. What is the general shape of the tree? Do the lower branches come off at the same angle as the upper? If untrimmed, what can you see of the trunk? Do the lower branches rest upon the ground? What advantage would this be to the tree in winter? Do the twigs stand out, or droop from the branches? Of what advantage is this in case of heavy snow? What is the color of the foliage? Where did the Norway spruce come from?

2. What is the color of the twig? How are the leaves set upon it? Are there more leaves on the upper than on the under side of the twigs of this year's growth? Of last year's growth? Brush your hand along a branch toward the tip. Do the leaves prick? Brush from the tip backward. Is the result the same? Why is this angle of the leaves to the twig a benefit during snowstorms?

3. Take a single leaf. What is its shape? How many sides has it? Is it soft or stiff? Is it sharp at the tip? Describe the buds which are forming for next year's growth. Look along the twigs and see if you can discov-

er the scales of the bud which produced last year's growth?

4. Where are the cones borne? How long does it take a cone to grow? Is it heavy? Is there resin on it? Note that the scales are set in a spiral around the center of the cone. Wind a string around a cone following the same row of scales. How many rows between those marked with a string? Look into the tip of a cone and see the spiral arrangement. Sketch and describe a cone-scale, paying special attention to the shape of the tip. Try to tear a cone apart. Is this easily done? Hang a closed cone in a dry place and note what happens.

Norway spruce seeds and samaras

5. Describe the seed, its wings and where it is placed at the base of the scale. How many seeds under each scale? When do the cones open of themselves to scatter the seed? Do you observe squirrels tearing these apart to get the seed?

6. The Norway spruce blossoms in May. Find the little flower which will produce the cone, and describe it. What color is it? Is it upright or hanging down? Do the scales turn toward the tip or backward? Why is this? Where are the pollen-catkins borne? How many of them arise from the same place on the twig? Can you see the little scales at the base of each pistillate catkin? What are they? Are they very full of pollen? Do the insects carry the pollen for the Norway spruce, or does the wind sift it over the pistillate blossoms? After the pollen is shed, note if the scales of the young cones close up. How long before the cones begin to droop? Do you think it is their weight which causes them to droop?

7. What use do we make of the Norway spruce? What is it used for in Europe?

> "All outward wisdom yields to that within,
>   Whereof nor creed nor canon holds the key;
> We only feel that we have ever been
>   And evermore shall be.
>
> And thus I know, by memories unfurled
>   In rarer moods, and many a nameless sign,
> That once in Time, and somewhere in the world,
>   I was a towering pine.
>
> Rooted upon a cape that overhung
>   The entrance to a mountain gorge; whereon
> The wintry shade of a peak was flung,
>   Long after rise of sun.
>
> There did I clutch the granite with firm feet,
>   There shake my boughs above the roaring gulf,
> When mountain whirlwinds through the passes beat,
>   And howled the mountain wolf.
>
> There did I louder sing than all the floods
>   Whirled in white foam adown the precipice,
> And the sharp sleet that stung the naked woods,
>   Answer with sullen hiss.
>
> I held the eagle till the mountain mist
>   Rolled from the azure paths he came to soar,
> And like a hunter, on my gnarled wrist
>   The dappled falcon bore."
>   —FROM "THE SPIRIT OF THE PINE," BAYARD TAYLOR.

White pine
Pitch pine

Norway spruce
Hemlock

The Hemlock

"O'er lonely lakes that wild and nameless lie,
Black, shaggy, vast and still as Barca's sands
A hemlock forest stands. Oh forest like a pall!
Oh hemlock of the wild, Oh brother of my soul
I love thy mantle black, thy shaggy bole,
Thy form grotesque, thy spreading arms of steel."

—PATTEE.

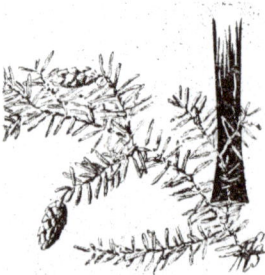

N its prime, the hemlock is a magnificent tree. It reaches the height of from sixty to one hundred feet, is cone-shaped, its fine, dense foliage and its drooping branches giving to its appearance exquisite delicacy; and I have yet to see elsewhere such graceful tree-spires as are the hemlocks of the Sierras, albeit they have bending tips. However, an old hemlock becomes very ragged and rugged in appearance; and dying, it rears its wind-broken branches against the sky, a gaunt figure of stark loneliness.

198

The hemlock branches are seldom broken by snow; they droop to let the burden slide off. The bark is reddish, or sometimes gray, and is furrowed into wide, scaly ridges. The foliage is a rich dark green, but whitish when seen from below. The leaves of the hemlock are really arranged in a spiral, but this is hard to demonstrate. They look as though they were arranged in double rows along each side of the little twig; but they are not in the same plane and there is usually a row of short leaves on the upper side of the twig. The leaf is blunt at the tip and has a little petiole of its own which distinguishes it from the leaves of any other species of conifer; it is dark, glossy green above, pale green beneath, marked with two white, lengthwise lines. In June, the tip of every twig grows and puts forth new leaves which are greenish yellow in color, making the tree very beautiful and giving it the appearance of blossoming. The leaves are shed during the third year. The hemlock cones are small and are borne on the tips of the twigs. The seeds are borne, two beneath each scale, and they have wings nearly as large as the scale itself. Squirrels are so fond of them that probably but few have an opportunity to try their wings. The cones mature in one year, and usually fall in the spring. The hemlock blossoms in May; the pistillate flowers are very difficult to observe as they are tiny and greenish and are placed at the tip of the twig. The pollen-bearing flowers are little, yellowish balls on delicate, short stems, borne along the sides of the twig.

Hemlock bark is rich in tannin and is used in great quantities for the tanning of leather. The timber, which is coarse-grained, is stiff and is used in framing buildings and for railroad ties; nails and spikes driven into it cling with great tenacity and the wood does not split in nailing. Oil distilled from the leaves of hemlock is used as an antiseptic.

The dense foliage of the hemlock offers a shelter to birds of all kinds in winter; even the partridges roost in the young trees. These young trees often have branches drooping to the ground, making an evergreen tent which forms a winter harbor for mice and other beasties. The seed-eating birds which remain with us during the winter, feed upon the seeds; and as the cones grow on the tips of the delicate twigs, the red squirrels display their utmost powers as acrobats when gathering this, their favorite food.

LESSON

Leading thought— This is one of the most common and useful and beautiful of our evergreen trees. Its fine foliage makes it an efficient winter shelter for birds.

Method—Ask the children the questions and request them to make notes on the hemlock trees of the neighborhood. The study of the leaves and the cones may be made in the schoolroom.

Observations—

1. Where does the hemlock tree grow in your neighborhood? What is the general shape of the tree? What sort of bark has it? How tall does it grow? How are its branches arranged to shed the snow?

2. What is the color of the foliage? How are the leaves arranged on the twigs? Are all the leaves of about the same size? What is the position of the smaller leaves?

3. Break off a leaf and describe its shape; its petiole. Does the leaf of any other evergreen have a petiole? What is the color and marking of the hemlock leaf above? Below? At what time of year are the new leaves developed? How does the hemlock tree look at this time? Does the hemlock ever shed its leaves?

4. Are the hemlock cones borne on the tip of the twigs or along the side? How long does it take a cone to mature? When does it fall? How many scales has it? Where are the seeds borne? How many seeds beneath each scale? Describe and sketch a hemlock seed. How are the seeds scattered? Study the tree in May, and see if you can find the blossom.

5. Make drawings of the following: The hemlock twig, showing the arrangement of the leaves; single leaf, enlarged; cone; cone scale; seed.

6. What creatures feed upon the hemlock seed? What birds find protection in the hemlock foliage in winter?

7. For what purposes is hemlock bark used? What is the timber good for? Is a nail easily pulled out from a hemlock board?

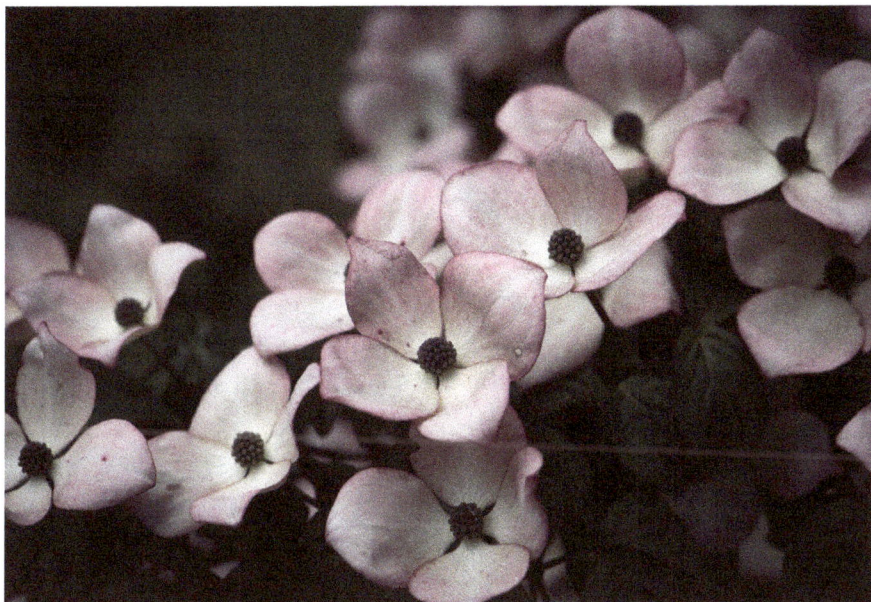

The flowers of a dogwood

The Dogwood

Through cloud rifts the sunlight is streaming in floods to far depths of the wood,
Retouching the velvet-leafed dogwood to crimson as vital as blood.

HERE is no prettier story among the flowers than that of the bracts of the dogwood, and it is a subject for investigation which any child can work out for himself. I shall never forget the thrill of triumph I experienced when I discovered for myself the cause of the mysterious dark notch at the tip of each great white bract, which I had for years idly noticed. One day my curiosity mastered my inertia, and I hunted a tree over for a flower bud, for it was rather late in the season; finally I was rewarded by finding the bracts in all stages of development.

The flowering dogwood forms its buds during the summer, and of course they must have winter protection; therefore, they are wrapped

in four, close-clasping, purplish brown scales, one pair inside and one pair outside, both thick and well fitted to protect the bunch of tiny flower buds at their center. But when spring comes, these motherly bud-scales change their duties, and by rapid growth become four beautiful white or pinkish bracts calling aloud to all the insect world that here at their hearts is something

Blossom and bud of a dogwood, enlarged

sweet. For months they brood the flowers and then display them to an admiring world. The artistic eye loves the little notch at the tip of the bracts, even before it has read in it the story of winter protection, of which it is an evidence.

The study of the flowers at the center is more interesting if aided by a lens. Within each blossom can be seen its tube, set in the four-lobed calyx. It has four slender petals curled back, its four chubby, greenish yellow anthers set on filaments which lift them up between the petals; and at the center of all is the tiny green pistil. There may be twenty, more or less, of these perfect flowers in this tiny, greenish yellow bunch at the center of the four great, flaring bracts. These flowers do not open simultaneously, and the yellow buds and open flowers are mingled together in the rosette. The calyx shows better on the bud than on the open flower. It might be well to explain to the pupils that a bract is simply a leaf in some other business than that ordinarily performed by leaves.

The twigs have a beautiful, smooth bark, purplish brown above and greenish below. The flowers grow at the tips of the twigs; and the young leaves are just below the flowers and also at the tips of the twigs. These twigs are spread and bent in a peculiar way, so that each white flower-head may be seen by the admiring world and not be hidden behind any of its neighbors. This habit makes this tree a favorite for planting, since it forms a mass of white bloom.

The dogwood banners unfurl before the flowers at their hearts open, and they remain after the last flower has received within itself the gracious, vital pollen which will enable it to mature into a beautiful berry. This long period of bloom is another quality which adds to the value of the dogwood as an ornamental tree. At the time the bracts fall, the curly petals also fall out leaving the little calyx-tubes standing with style and stigma projecting from their centers, making them look like a bunch of liliputian churns with dashers. In autumn, the foliage turns to a rich, purplish crimson—a most satisfying color.

During the winter, the flowering dogwood, which renders our forests so beautiful in early spring, may be readily recognized by its bark, which is broken up into small scales and mottled like the skin of a serpent; and on the tips of its branches are the beautiful clusters of red berries, or speaking more exactly, drupes. This fruit is oval, with a brilliant, shining, red, pulpy covering which must be attractive to birds. At its tip it has a little purple crown, in the center of which may be seen the remnant of the style, but this attractive outside covers a seed with a very thick, hard shell, which is quite indigestible and fully able to protect, even from the attack of the digestive juices of the bird's stomach, the tender white kernel within it, which includes the stored food and the embryo. There are in the North two other common species of dogwood which have dark blue fruit.

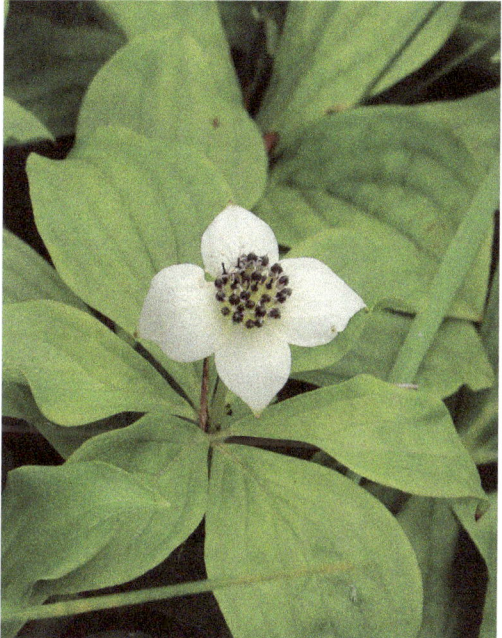

DOMINICUS JOHANNES BERGSMA (CC BY-SA 3.0)
Dwarf cornel or bunchberry — a dwarf dogwood

LESSON

Leading thought— The petals are not the only means of attracting insects to the flowers. Sometimes other parts of the plant are made into banners to show insects where the nectar is to be found.

The flower buds of the dogwood are formed during the previous season

Method— Bring in a branch of the dogwood when it is in flower. The branch should have upon it some flowers that are unopened. Study the flower first, and ask the pupils to discover for themselves why the great white bracts have a notch in the tip. A lens is a great help to the interest in studying these tiny flowers.

Observations—

1. What is there at the center of the dogwood flower? How do the parts at the center look? Are they of the same shape? Are some opened and others not? Take a penknife and cut out one that is opened and describe it. Can you see how many petals this tiny flower has? Describe its calyx. How many stamens has it? Can you see the pistil? If a flower has a calyx and stamens and a pistil, has it not all that a flower needs?

2. How many of these flowers are there at the center of the dogwood "blossom"? What color are they? Would they show off much if it were not for the great white banners around them? Do we not think of these great white bracts as the dogwood flower?

3. Study one of these banners. What is its shape? Are the four white bracts the same shape and size? Make a sketch of these four bracts with the bunch of flowers at the center. What is there peculiar about each one of these white bracts. Why should this notch be there? Find one of the flower-heads which is not yet opened and watch it develop, and then write a little story of the work done in the winter for the flowers by these bracts and the different work done by them in the spring, all for the sake of the precious blossoms.

4. Sketch the bracts from below. Is one pair wider than the other? Is the wider pair inside or outside? Why is this so?

5. Where are the flowers of the dogwood borne? How are the twigs arranged so as to unfurl all the banners and not hide one behind another, so that the whole tree is a mass of white?

6. While studying the flowers, study where the young leaves come from. Can you still see the scales which protected the leaf buds?

7. What kind of fruit develops from the dogwood blossoms? What colors are its leaves in autumn?

Dogwoods line a path

The fall leaves of a sumac

The Velvet, or Staghorn, Sumac

TEACHER'S STORY

The sumacs with flame leaves at half-mast,
like wildfire spread over the glade;
Above them, the crows on frayed pinions
move northward in ragged parade.

 HE sumacs, in early autumn, form a "firing line" along the borders of woodlands and fences, before any other plant but the Virginia creeper has thought of taking on brighter colors. No other leaves can emulate the burning scarlet of their hues. The sumacs are a glory to our hills; and sometime, when Americans have time to cultivate a true artistic sense, these shrubs will play an important part in landscape gardening. They are beautiful in summer, when each crimson "bob" (a homely New England name for the fruit panicle) is set at

the center of the bouquet of spreading, fernlike leaves. In winter nakedness they are most picturesque, with their broadly branching twigs bearing aloft the wine-colored pompons against the background of snow, and calling to the winter birds to come and partake of the pleasantly acid drupes. In spring, they put out their soft leaves in exquisite shades of pale pinkish green, and when in blossom their staminate panicles of greenish white cover them with loose pyramids of delicate bloom.

a. Pistillate flower from a "bob."
b. Staminate flower from the greenish panicle.

Well may it be called velvet sumac, for this year's growth of wood and the leaf stems are covered with fine hairs, pinkish at first, but soon white; if we slip our fingers down a branch, we can tell even without looking where last year's growth began and ended, because of the velvety feel. The name staghorn sumac is just as fitting, for its upper branches spread widely like a stag's horns and, like them, the new growth is covered with velvet.

The leaves are borne on the new wood, and therefore at the ends of branches; they are alternate; the petiole broadens where it clasps the branch, making a perfect nursery for the little next-year's bud, which is nestled below it. The leaves are compound and the number of leaflets varies from eleven to thirty-one. Each leaflet is set close to the midrib, with a base that is not symmetrical; the leaflets have their edges toothed, and are long and narrow; they do not spread out on either side the midrib like a fern, but naturally droop somewhat, and thus conceal their undersides, which are much lighter in color. The leaflets are not always set exactly opposite; the basal ones are bent back toward the main stem, making a fold in the base of each. The end leaflets are not always three, symmetrically set, but sometimes are two and sometimes one, with two basal lobes.

The wine-colored "bob" is cone-shaped, but with a bunchy surface. Remove all the seeds from it and note its framework of tiny branches, and again pay admiring tribute to nature's way of doing up compact packages. Each seed is a drupe, as is also the cherry. A drupe is merely a seed within a fleshy layer, all being enclosed in a firmer outside covering; here, the outside case is covered with dark red fuzz, a clothing of furs for winter, the fur standing out in all directions. The fleshy part around the seed has a pleasantly acid taste, and one of my childhood diversions was to share these fruits in winter with the birds. I probably inadvertently ate also many a little six-footed brother hidden away for winter safe-keeping, for every sumac panicle is a crowded insect-tenement.

It is only in its winter aspect that we can see the peculiar way of the sumac's branching, which is in picturesque zigzags, ending with coarse, wide-spreading twigs. As each terminal twig was a stem for the bouquet of blossom and fruit set about with graceful leaves, it needed room and this is reason enough for the coarse branching. The wood of the sumac has a pith, and is coarse in texture.

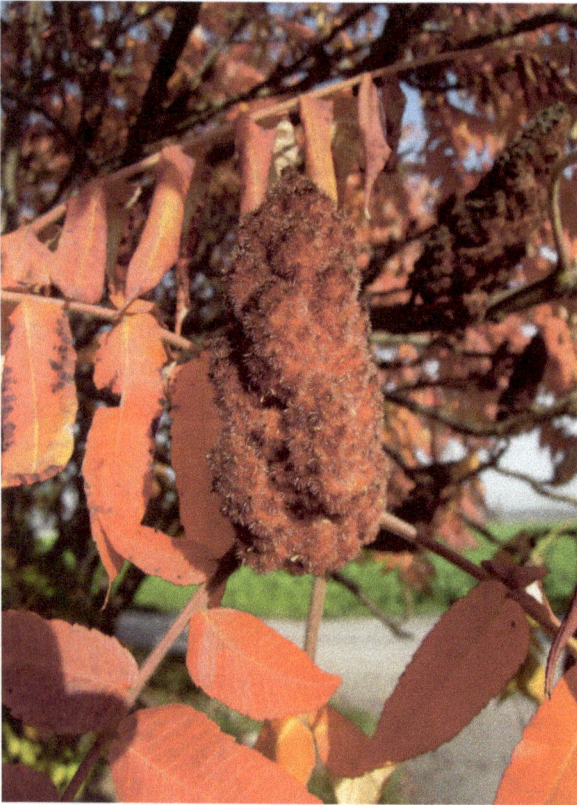

Staghorn sumac

During late May the new growth starts near the end of last year's twig; the buds are yellowish and show off against the dark gray twigs. From the center of these buds comes the fuzzy new growth, which is usually reddish purple; the tiny leaves are folded, each leaflet creased at its midrib and folded tightly against itself; as the leaves unfold, they are olive-green tinted with red, and look like tassels coming out around the old dark red "bob." When the sumacs are in blossom, we see in every group of them, two kinds; one with pyramids of white flowers, and the other with pinkish callow bobs. The structure of these two different flower-clusters is really the same, except that the white ones are looser and more widely spread. Each flower of the white panicle is staminate, and has five greenish, somewhat hairy sepals and five yellowish white petals, at the center of which are five large anthers. A flower from the bob is quite different; it has the five hairy sepals alternating with five narrow, yellowish white petals, both clasping the globular base, or ovary, which is now quite covered with pinkish plush, and bears at its tip the three styles flaring into stigmas.

The velvet sumac is larger than the smooth species (*Rhus glabra*), and is easily distinguished from it, since the new wood of the latter is smooth and covered with bloom but is not at all velvety. The poison sumac, which is very dangerous to many people when handled, is a swamp species and its fruit is a loose, drooping panicle of whitish berries, very much like that of poison ivy; therefore, any sumac that has the red bob is not dangerous. The poison species has the edges of its leaflets entire and each leaflet has a distinct petiole of its own where it joins the midrib.

There is much tannin in sumac and it is used extensively to tan leather. The bobs are used for coloring a certain shade of brown. The famous Japanese lacquer is made from the juice of a species of sumac.

LESSON

Leading thought— The sumac is a beautiful shrub in summer because of its fern-like leaves; it is picturesque in winter, and its colors in autumn are most brilliant. Its dark red fruit clusters remain upon it during the entire winter. In June it shows two kinds of blossoms on different shrubs, one is whitish and bears the pollen, the other is reddish and is a pistillate flower, later developing into the seed on the "bob" or fruit cluster.

Method— Begin this study in October when the beautiful autumn color of the leaves attracts the eye. Observations to be made in the field should be outlined and should be answered in the field notebooks. The study of the fruit and leaf may be made in the schoolroom, and an interest should be developed which will lead to the study of the interesting flowers the following spring. The sumacs in autumn make a beautiful subject for watercolor sketches, and their peculiar method of branching with their dark red seed clusters or bobs, make them excellent subjects for winter sketching.

Observations—

1. Why is this called the velvet sumac? Why is it called the staghorn sumac? Look at the stems with a lens and describe the velvet. Can you tell this year's wood by the velvet? Is there any velvet on last year's wood? Is there any on the wood below? What is there peculiar in the appearance of last year's wood? What are the colors of the hairs that make the velvet on this year's growth? On last year's growth? What is the color of this year's growth under the velvet? Where are the leaves borne?

2. Look at the leaves. How many come off the stem between two, one of which is above the other? Is the midrib velvety? What is its color at base and at tip? What is the shape of the petiole where it joins the stem? Remove the leaf. What do you find hidden and protected by its broad base?

3. How many leaflets are there on the longest leaf which you can find? How many on the shortest? Do the leaflets have little petioles, or are they set close to the midrib? How does the basal pair differ from the others? Are the leaflets the same color above as below? Are the pairs set exactly opposite each other? Look at the three leaflets at the tips of several leaves and see if they are all regular in form. Draw a leaflet showing its base, its veins and its margin. Draw an entire leaf, and color it as exactly as possible.

4. Study the fruit. Pick one of the bobs and note its general shape. Is it smooth or bunchy? Sketch it. Remove one of the little bunches and find out why it is of that shape. Remove all of the seeds from one of last year's bobs and see how the fruit is borne. Sketch a part of such a bare stem.

5. Take a single seed; look at it through a lens and describe it. What are the colors? Cut or pare away the flesh, and describe the seed. What birds live on the sumac seeds in winter? How many kinds of insects can you find wintering in the bob? Find a seed free from insects and taste it.

Winter Study of the Sumac—

6. Study the sumac after the leaves have fallen and sketch it. What

is there peculiar in its branching? Of what use to the plant is its method of branching? Break a branch and look at the end. Is there a pith? What color is the wood and pith?

May or June Study of the Sumac—

Staghorn sumac

7. Where on the branch does the new growth start? How are the tiny leaves folded? Look over a group of sumacs and see if their blossoms all look alike. Are the different kinds of blossoms found on the same tree or on different trees? Take one of the white pyramidal blossom clusters; look at one of these flowers with a lens and describe its sepals and petals. How many anthers has it and where are they? This is a pollen-bearing flower and has no pistil. How are its tiny staminate flowers arranged on the stem to give the beautiful pyramid shape? This kind of flower cluster is called a panicle.

8. Take one of the green bobs and see if it is made up of little round flowers. Through a lens study one of these. How many sepals? How many petals? Describe the middle of the flower around which the petals and sepals clasp. Is this the ovary, or seed box? Can you see the stigmas protruding beyond it? What insects visit these flowers?

9. How can you tell the velvet or staghorn sumac from the smooth sumac? How can you tell both of these from the poison sumac?

10. To what uses are the sumacs put?

"I see the partridges feed quite extensively upon the sumach berries, at my old house. They come to them after every snow, making fresh tracks, and have now stripped many bushes quite bare."

—THOREAU'S JOURNAL, FEB. 4, 1856.

A witch-hazel (foreground) with carious hemlocks, hardwoods, and several white birches (far right)

The Witch-Hazel

In the dusky, somber woodland, thwarting vistas dull and cold,
Thrown in vivid constellations, gleam the hazel stars of gold,
Gracious gift of wealth untold.

Hazel blossoms brightly glowing through the forests dark and drear,
Work sweet miracles, bestowing gladness on the dying year,
Joy of life in woods grown sere.

WITCH-HAZEL is not only a most interesting shrub in itself, but it has connected with it many legends. From its forked twigs were made the divining rods by which hidden springs of water or mines of precious metals were found, as it was firmly believed that the twig would turn in the hand when the one who held it passed over the spring or mine. At the present day, its fresh leaves and twigs are used in large quantities for the distilling of the healing extract so much in demand as a remedy for cuts and bruises and for chapped or sunburned skins. It is said that the Oneida Indians first taught the white people concerning its medicinal qualities.

The witch-hazel is a large shrub, usually from six to twelve feet high, although under very advantageous circumstances it has been known to take a tree-like form and attain a height of more than twenty feet. Its bark

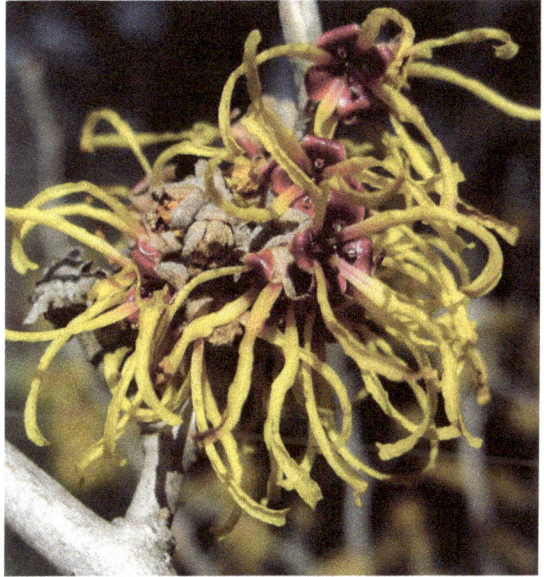

Witch-hazel blossoms

is very dark grayish brown, smooth, specked with little dots, which are the lenticels, or breathing-pores. If the season's growth has been rapid, the new twigs are lighter in color, but when stunted by drouth or poor soil, the new growth has a tint similar to the old. The wood is white, very tough and fibrous, with a pith or heart-wood of softer substance and yellow in color. The leaves are alternate, and the leaf buds appear at the tips of the season's twigs, while the blossoms grow at the axils of the leaves.

The witch-hazel leaf is nearly as broad as it is long, bluntly pointed at its tip, with a stem generally less than one-half inch in length. The sides are unequal in size and shape, and the edges are roughly scalloped. The veins are straight, are depressed on the upper side but very prominent beneath, and they are lighter in color than the rest of the leaf. Witch-hazel leaves are likely to be apartment houses for insects, especially the insects that make galls. Of these there are many species, each making a different shaped gall. One of the most common is a gall, shaped like a little horn or spur on the upper side of the leaf and having a tiny door opening on the under side of the leaf. If one of these snug little homes is torn open, it will be found occupied by a community of little aphids, or plant-lice.

The witch-hazel blossoms appear at the axil of a leaf or immediately above the scar from which a leaf has fallen, the season of bloom being so late that often the bush is bare of leaves and is clothed only with the yellow, fringe-like flowers. Usually the flowers are in clusters of three, but occasionally four or five can be found on the same very short stem. The calyx is four-lobed, the petals are four in number, shaped like tiny, yellow ribbons, about one-half inch long and not much wider than a coarse thread. In the bud, these petals are rolled inward in a close spiral, like a watch-spring, and are coiled so tightly that each bud is a solid little ball no larger than a bird-shot. There are four stamens lying between the petals, and between each two of these stamens is a little scale just opposite the petal. The anthers are most interesting. Each has two little doors which fly open, as if by magic springs, and throw out the pollen which clings to them. The pistil has two stigmas, which are joined above the two-celled seed-box, or ovary. The blossoms sometimes open in late September, but the greater number appear in October and November. They are more beautiful in November after the leaves have fallen, since these yellow, starry flowers seem to bring light and warmth into the landscape. After the petals fall, the calyx forms a beautiful little urn, holding the growing fruit.

The nuts seem to require a sharp frost to separate the closely joined parts; it requires a complete year to mature them. One of these nuts is about half an inch long and is covered with a velvety green outer husk, until the frost turns it brown; cutting through it discloses a yellowish white inner shell, which is as hard as bone; within this are the

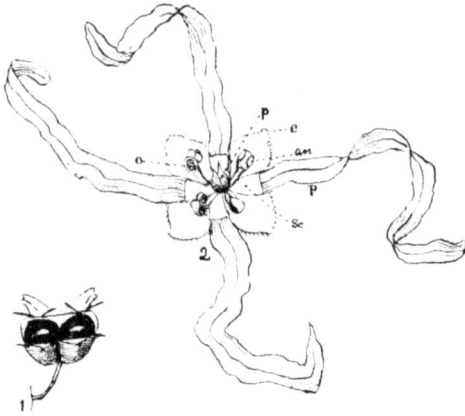

1, A queer little face—witch-hazelnut ready to shoot its seeds. 2, Enlarged flower of witch-hazel showing the long petals; p, with dotted line the pistil; an, anther; a, anther with doors open; c, lobes of calyx; sc, scale opposite the base of petal.

two brown seeds each ornamented with a white dot; note particularly that these seeds lie in close-fitting cells. The fruit, if looked at when the husk is opening, bears an odd resemblance to a grotesque monkey-like face with staring eyes. Frosty nights will open the husks, and the dry warmth of sunny days or of the heated schoolroom, will cause the edges of the cups which hold the seeds, to curve inward with such force as to send the seeds many feet away; ordinarily they are thrown from ten to twenty feet, but Hamilton Gibson records one actual measurement of forty-five feet. The children should note that the surface of the seeds is very polished and smooth, and the way they are discharged may be likened to that by which an orange seed is shot from between the fingers.

LESSON

Leading thought— The witch-hazel blossoms during the autumn, and thus adds beauty to the landscape. It has an interesting mechanism by which it can shoot its seeds for a distance of many feet.

Method— This lesson divides naturally into two parts; a study of the way the seeds are distributed is fitted for the primary grades, and a study of the flower for more advanced grades.

KATJA SCHULZ (CC BY 2.0)
Young witch-hazel fruit

For the primary grades the lesson should begin by the gathering of the twigs which bear the fruit. These should be brought to the schoolroom—there to await results. Soon the seeds will be popping all over the schoolroom, and then the question as to how this is done, and why, may be made the topic of the lesson. For the study of the flower and the shrub itself, the work should begin in October when the blossoms are still in bud. As they expand they may be studied, a lens being necessary for observing the interesting little doors to the anthers.

Leaves, fruits, and blossoms of witch hazel. Various types of galls, and the work of miners can be seen on the leaves

1. Is the witch-hazel a shrub or a tree?

2. What is the color of the bark? Is it thick or thin, rough or smooth, dark or light, or marked with dots or lines? Is there any difference in color between the older wood and the young twigs? Is the wood tough or brittle? Dark or light in color?

3. Do the leaves grow opposite each other or alternate? On what part of the plant do the leaf buds grow?

4. What is the general shape of the leaf? Is it more pointed at the base or at the tip? Are the leaves regular in form, or larger on one side than the other? Are the edges entire, toothed, or wavy? Are the petioles short or long? Are the veins straight or branching? Are they prominent? Are the leaves of the same color on both sides?

5. Are there many queer-shaped little swellings on the leaf above and below? See how many of these you can find. Tell what you think they are.

6. Do the flowers grow singly or in clusters? What is the shape and color of the petals, and how many of them are there in each blossom? Describe the calyx. If there are any flower buds just opening, observe and describe the way the petals are folded within them.

7. How many stamens? With a lens observe the way the two little doors to the anther fly open; how is the pollen thrown out? What is the shape of the pistil? How many stigmas?

8. Does each individual flower have a stem or is there a common

stem for a cluster of blossoms? Do the flowers grow at the tips or along the sides of the twigs? When do the witch-hazel flowers appear and how long do they last?

9. Make a drawing of a witch-hazel nut before it opens. What is the color of the outer husk when ripe? Cut into a closed nut and observe the extreme hardness and strength of the inner shell.

10. Where are the seeds situated? Can you see that

Witch-hazel flowering in a park

the shell, when partially open, ready to throw out the seeds, resembles a queer little face? Describe the color and marking of the seeds; are they rough or smooth? How far have you known the witch-hazel to throw its seeds? Study the nut and try to discover how it throws the seeds so far.

References—*Tree Book*, Rogers; *Our Northern Shrubs*, Keeler; *Familiar Trees and Their Leaves*, Mathews; *Field, Forest and Wayside Botany*, Gray.

The Mountain Laurel

TEACHER'S STORY

S a child I never doubted that the laurel wreaths of Grecian heroes were made from mountain laurel, and I supposed, of course, that the flowers were used also. My vision was of a hero crowned with huge wreaths of laurel bouquets, which I thought so beautiful. It was a shock to exchange this sumptuous headgear of my dreams for a plain wreath of leaves from the green-bay tree.

However, the mountain laurel leaf is evergreen and beautiful enough to crown a victor; in color it is a rich, lustrous green above, with a yellow midrib, the lower side being of a much lighter color. In shape, the leaf is long, narrow, pointed at each end and smooth-edged, with a rather short petiole. The leaves each year grow on the new wood, which is greenish and rough, in contrast with the old wood, which is rich brownish red. The leaves are arranged below the flower cluster, so that they make a shining green base for this natural bouquet.

The flowers grow on the tips of the branching twigs, which are huddled together in a manner that brings into a mass many flowers.

Diagram of flower of laurel
p, pocket; st, stamen

I have counted seventy-five of them in a single bunch; the youngest flowers grow nearest the tip of the twig. The blossom stems are pink, and afford a rich background for the starry open flowers and knobby closed buds. The bud of the laurel blossom is very pretty and resembles a bit of rose-colored pottery; it has a five-sided, pyramidal top, and at the base of the pyramid are ten little buttresses which flare out from the calyx. The calyx is five-lobed, each lobe being green at the base and pink at the point. Each one of the ten little buttresses or ridges is a groove in which a stamen is growing, as we may see by looking into an opening flower; each anther is "headed" toward the pocket which ends the groove. The filament lengthens and shoves the anther into the pocket, and then keeps on growing until it forms a bow-shaped spring, like a sapling with the top bent to the ground. The opening flower is saucerlike, pinkish white, and in form is a five-pointed star. At the bottom of the saucer a ten-pointed star is outlined in crimson; and bowed above this crimson ring are the ten white filaments with their red-brown anthers stuffed cozily into the pockets, one pocket at the center of each lobe, and one half-way between; each pocket is marked with a splash of crimson with spotty edges. From the center of the flower projects the stigma, far from and above the pollen-pockets.

Each laurel flower is thus set with ten spring-traps all awaiting the visit of the unwary moth or bee which, when seeking the nectar at the center of the flower, is sure to touch one or all of these bent filaments. As soon as one is touched, up it springs and slings its pollen hard at the intruder. The pollen is not simply a shower of powder, but is in the form of a sticky string, as if the grains were strung on cobweb silk. When liberating these springs with a pencil point, I have seen the pollen thrown a distance of thirteen inches; thus, if the pollen ammunition does not strike the bee, it may fall upon some open flower in the neighborhood. The anthers spring back after this performance and the filaments curl over each other at the center of the flower below the pink stigma; but after a few hours they straighten out and each empty anther is suspended above its own pocket. The anthers open while in the pocket, each one is slit open at its tip so that it is like the leather pocket of a sling.

Leaves and early buds of mountain laurel

After the corollas fall, the long stigma still projects from the tip of the ripening ovary, and there it stays, until the capsule is ripe and open. The five-pointed calyx remains as an ornamental cup for the fruit. The capsule opens along five valves, and each section is stuffed with little, almost globular seeds.

The mountain laurel grows in woods and shows a preference for rocky mountain sides or sandy soil.

Another of the common species is the sheep laurel, which grows in swampy places, especially on hillsides. The flowers of this are smaller and pinker than the mountain laurel, and are set below the leaves on the twig. Another species called the pale, or swamp, laurel, has very small flowers, not more than half an inch in breadth and its leaves have rolled-back edges and are whitish green beneath. This species is found only in cold peat-bogs and swamps.

LESSON

Leading thought— The laurel blossom is set with ten springs, and each spring acts as a sling in throwing pollen upon visiting insects, thus making sure that the visitor will carry pollen to other waiting flowers.

Method— Have the pupils bring to the schoolroom a branch of laurel which shows blossoms in all stages from the bud. Although this lesson is on the mountain laurel, any of the other species will do as well.

Observations—

1. How are the laurel leaves set about the blossom clusters to make them beautiful? What is the shape of the laurel leaf? What are its colors above and below? How do the leaves grow with reference to the flowers? Do they grow on last year's or this year's wood? How can you tell the new wood from the old?

2. Take a blossom bud. What is its shape? How many sides to the pyramid-like tip? How many little flaring ridges at the base of the pyramid? Describe the calyx.

3. What is the shape of the flower when open? How many lobes has it? What is its color? Where is it marked with red?

4. In the open blossom, what do you see of the ten ridges, or keels, which you noticed in the bud? How does each one of these grooves end? What does the laurel blossom keep in these ten pockets? Touch one of the ten filaments with a pencil and note what happens.

5. Take a bud scarcely open. Where are the stamens? Can you see the anthers? Take a blossom somewhat more open. Where are the anthers now? From these observations explain how the stamens place their anthers in the pockets. How do the filaments grow into bent springs?

6. Are the anthers open when they are still in the pocket? Look at an anther with a lens and tell how many slits it has. How do they open? Are the pollen grains loose when they are thrown from the anther? How are they fastened together? Does this pollen mass stick to whatever it touches?

7. What is the use to the flower of this arrangement for throwing pollen? What insects set free the stamen-springs? Where is the nectar which the bee or moth is after? Can it get this nectar without setting free the springs? Touch the filaments with a pencil and see how far they will sling the pollen.

8. Describe the pistil in the open flower. Is the stigma near the anthers? Would they be likely to throw their pollen on the stigma of their own flower? Could they throw it on the stigmas of neighboring flowers?

9. How does the fruit of the laurel look? Does the style still cling after the corolla falls? Describe the fruit-capsule. How does it open? How do the seeds look? Are there many of them?

10. Where does the mountain laurel grow? What kind of soil does it like? Do you know any other species of laurel? If so, are they found in the same situations as the mountain laurel?

"A childish gladness stays my feet,
　　As through the winter woods I go,
Behind some frozen ledge to meet
　　A kalmia shining through the snow.

I see it, beauteous as it stood
　　Ere autumn's glories paled and fled,
And sigh no more in pensive mood,
　　'My leafy oreads are all dead.'

I hear its foliage move, like bells
　　On rosaries strung, and listening there,
Forget the icy wind that tells
　　Of turfless fields, and forests bare.

All gently with th' inclement scene
　　I feel its glossy verdure blend;—
I bless that lovely evergreen
　　As heart in exile hails a friend.

Its boughs, by tempest scarcely stirred,
　　Are tents beneath whose emerald fold
The rabbit and the snowbound bird
　　Forget the world is white and cold.

And still, 'mid ruin undestroyed,
　　Queen arbor with the fadeless crown,
Its brightness warms the frosty void,
　　And softens winter's surliest frown."

—FROM "THE MOUNTAIN LAUREL," THERON BROWN.

www.ingramcontent.com/pod-product-compliance
Lightning Source LLC
Chambersburg PA
CBHW051244020426
42333CB00025B/3052